Teach Like a Techie

Teach Like a Techie

20 Tools for Reaching the Digital Generation

LORI ELLIOTT, EdD

"The Accidental Techie"

Crystal Springs
SDE BOOKS

A division of Staff Development for Educators

Peterborough, New Hampshire

Published by Crystal Springs Books
A division of Staff Development for Educators (SDE)
10 Sharon Road, PO Box 500
Peterborough, NH 03458
1-800-321-0401
www.SDE.com/crystalsprings

Published 2011
Printed in the United States of America
15 14 13 12 11   1 2 3 4 5

ISBN: 978-1-935502-09-8

Library of Congress Cataloging-in-Publication Data

Elliott, Lori, 1968-
    Teach like a techie : 20 tools for reaching the digital generation /
Lori Elliott.
        p.   cm.
    Includes bibliographical references and index.
    ISBN 978-1-935502-09-8
    1. Internet in education.   2. Educational technology.   3. Digital
media. I. Title.
    LB1044.87.E438 2011
    371.33—dc22
                                                        2011011311

Editor: Diane Lyons
Art Director and Designer: Jill Shaffer Hammond
Cover Design: Tamara English, Bill Smith Group
Robot Illustrations: Bruce Hammond
Production Coordinator: Deborah Fredericks

This book is dedicated to
my incredibly supportive husband and best friend, Tim;
and my hilarious and talented children, Austin and Ashlyn.
Your love, patience, and encouragement made this book possible.

Contents

Acknowledgments

Writing a book has always been a personal goal of mine. I'm forever grateful to Ed Milliken and Terra Tarango at Staff Development for Educators for giving me the opportunity to write my first book. I also want to thank Sharon Smith and Diane Lyons, my talented editors, for being so wonderful to work with. I really appreciate all the hours of hard work, genius rewrites and additions, and the fun communication along the way. You two are the best! And I'd like to extend a very special thanks to Jill Shaffer Hammond. Your design work has made the book look so attractive and inviting.

I couldn't do what I do without the support of my wonderful family. Their constant love and support have allowed me to grow and pursue my dreams. My parents, Larry and Linda Ferguson, have been my greatest cheerleaders. They've always believed in me and encouraged me to keep learning and sharing what I know with others. Even though Dad is gone now, I know he would be so proud of this book. Thanks, Mom, for always being there to listen and give me just the right advice. You showed me how to be strong and independent, and that has served me well over the years.

To my husband, Tim: you are truly my rock. Through all the years of my teaching long hours, getting yet another degree, traveling, and creating, you've been holding down the fort by running the kids wherever they needed to go, building the perfect home or awesome furniture for my classroom, and making us all laugh at the same time. I couldn't have a better mate.

To my amazing kids, Austin and Ashlyn: you make me so proud. You are both incredibly smart, creative, funny, talented, and caring. Ever since you guys were little, you just rolled with the punches, and I love that about you two! Your selflessness reminds me how to live, and your humor keeps me from taking things or myself too seriously. I am so honored to be your Mom.

Finally, I must send a huge thank you to the friends and colleagues of Nixa Public Schools. It's because of you that I've become the teacher I am today. I've had the tremendous pleasure of working with the finest educators in the country. Every administrator, teacher, and staff member has a passion for teaching and helping students succeed. What an awesome environment to teach and learn in! I have so many great memories of brainstorming, planning, working, and, yes, laughing together! I couldn't ask for better friends! A big thank you also goes to the students and parents I have had the pleasure of working with over the last 20 years. I've always felt we made a great team! Nixa Public Schools is and will always be my home, and you know what they say: "there's no place like home!"

Introduction

I'm a teacher by choice and a techie by accident. It's true. What I know about technology has come through my own journey to try and find new ways to reach my students. It wasn't that I really wanted to keep up with them; I've always been smart enough to know that they're ahead of me in this area, but rather I knew there were tools and resources out there that would make teaching and learning more meaningful and real.

My journey started about 20 years ago when I got my first teaching job. I was so excited. There weren't computers in the class-rooms yet, but we had a computer lab. We were thrilled to have a computer teacher because most of us on staff were clueless about computers. All I knew was that when I went to pick up my students from computer class, they had spent almost an hour playing some kind of educational game. They were either practicing multiplication facts by racing noisy cartoon cars on the screen or trying not to get bitten by a snake on the Oregon Trail. It was all about software back then, and schools dumped money into computers and educational software. I realized that I really didn't understand why or how to use this new technology that my students seemed to be very comfortable with.

Over the years I jumped head first into things I knew very little about. I remember when the Internet became available in all of our classrooms and when I attended my first e-mail training. It kind of scared me to think that my information would be out in space somewhere for anyone to see. I look at all the usernames and passwords I have now and laugh about my reservations back then. I have grown from truly not knowing how to plug in a computer to teaching in a technology-infused classroom with a SMART Board, 12 student computers, and lots of gadgets and gizmos. I even train teachers in my district and around the country how to enhance their instruction with technology tools. The teaching thing comes naturally; the techie thing is a work in progress. I still talk like a teacher and say things like "doohickey" to refer to certain buttons on the keyboard. My focus is not on terminology or trying to sound smart, but rather on students and their achievement. I want to understand how students learn and what tools I can use to engage them in meaningful ways.

> Do you know that brain experts really believe that our students' brains are actually wired differently from ours, those of us who did not grow up with all this technology?

Today's Learners

Are today's students really any different than earlier generations? I mean we've had technology in some form or fashion since the beginning of time. One definition of technology by Fitzgerald (2002) is "the application of knowledge and resources to meet human needs." Every time we need something to make our work easier or get something done, some device seems to be created. I like the way Mishra and Koehler discussed technology in 2009: "Technology is all the new stuff that appeared after we were born. The stuff that was around before we arrived on the planet, we often take for granted."

This definition is, in a nutshell, why today's students really are different from those of earlier decades. Think of all the "stuff" they've grown up with. They don't know a world without the Internet, cell phones, iPods, videos, and computers.

Larry Rosen (2010) puts it this way: "Today's children have grown up in an environment in which technology is everywhere, and much of it is invisible." He uses a toaster as an illustration for this idea. Do you really get up in the morning and stand in your kitchen in awe of the ability of the toaster to toast your bagel? I doubt it. You just know it does what you need it to do and you grew up with one, so who cares how the thing works. Students today feel the same way about technology. They aren't really wowed by the capability to be in constant contact with people all over the world or by being able to get information they need at a click of a button. So, yes this generation—the Digital Native—is different. Marc Prensky coined the term "Digital Natives" to refer to those born after 1980. These individuals have grown up in the digital world. He named those born before 1980 the "Digital Immigrants." These folks did not grow up with technology as an integral part of their everyday life.

Do you know that brain experts really believe that our students' brains are actually wired differently from ours, those of us who did not grow up with all this technology? Yes. Prensky, Jensen, and Tapscott have found that continued immersion in technology over time rewires the brain. The ability of the brain to reorganize or rewire itself is called neuroplasticity. Because of multi-tasking, social networking, and getting information in bursts during video games or from the Internet, the brain is rewiring itself. This is why you can hand your new iPhone to a four year old and, within minutes, she'll have it figured out and set up for you. You see to her, it works like everything else in the environment so it just makes sense.

Is This Engagement or Just Entertainment?

Scary, huh? There are, of course, concerns about this constant use of technology. How safe are online activities? What if students can't communicate or write properly? What if we lose common courtesies and social etiquette? Just as with any change in our culture, we'll have to lead and coach our students and children to use the tools appropriately. The bottom line is that technology is not going away, whether we like it or not. Many teachers get upset and say that bringing all this technology into the classroom is a waste of time because kids today just want to be entertained. Really? Is there a difference between entertainment and engagement?

> Technology doesn't teach. We do! The tools we choose to use in our classrooms to engage learners won't work without a strong understanding of best instructional practices and classroom management.

I've found that students aren't asking me to entertain them because, to be honest, my show wouldn't last long. I'm just not that funny or talented. No, I have found, and the research of Prensky and the national technology survey *Speak Up* has shown, that students want to be engaged in truly meaningful experiences. They want to know how and why the content will be used in their everyday lives or careers. If they're not engaged, then they're just playing the school game. It breaks my heart to hear high school kids talk about just getting through high school or as they put it, "jumping through hoops."

Technology doesn't teach. We do! The tools we choose to use in our classrooms to engage learners won't work without a strong understanding of best instructional practices and classroom management. Throwing a cool web tool at students without solid lesson plans, expectations, guidelines, modeling, practice, and assessment is really a waste of time. To teach like techies, we have to sharpen our teaching skills first and then turn to the technology tools for a little help. This book is designed to help you do both, with as little agonizing and as little investment of your time as possible.

One thing I know is that the keys to successful teaching and learning have remained the same. Positive student/teacher relationships and best instructional practices are still the foundation for success. You can have all the latest and greatest tech toys in your classroom, but if you don't know how to connect with students and present information in a meaningful way that students want to grab hold of, the technology is worthless.

If It Hasn't Changed Yet, Wait Five Minutes

Another thing I know is that technology (e.g., websites, equipment, online tools) changes rapidly, and we have to understand this when incorporating it into the classroom. However, good teaching methods have not changed, and scaffolding learning for students is necessary no matter what tool you're using. This book will present some of my favorite resources, but I'm very aware they'll change over time. So, the book is designed to not just highlight the tool, but focus on how to use it, the realities involved with using it, and what experts say about best practices. Even when we have moved on to new websites, apps, and devices, try to remember the lesson construction and classroom management tips as you apply them to the new tools.

> To teach like techies, we have to sharpen our teaching skills first and then turn to the technology tools for a little help.

A Quick User's Guide to This Book

This book is organized into three sections. The first shows you web tools that can enhance teaching; the second is all about today's hottest hardware; and the third shows you web tools that make everyone's life easier.

Each technology tool is explained step-by-step so you can understand how to start working with it right away. Detailed lesson ideas are given for every section. The lessons vary by grade, but the organization and best teaching practices can stretch across all grade levels K–12. I know you hate it when presenters tell you to adapt the lessons to your grade level, but with technology you really can. In K–2, you may want to use some of these tools in your instruction. Consider using your projector so all the students can participate at the same time by viewing the resource. In grades 3–8, or high school, you may be using the computer lab, mobile laptop cart, or homework assignment to put students to work using the tools discussed. Examine each of the 20 tools for ways you can use them in your classroom instruction and how students can use the tools themselves to enhance their learning.

> See where you stand on the Techie Continuum now, and then come back to it after you've been using this book for a while . . .

The book is also designed with your busy schedule in mind. Each chapter is set up to be read independently of the others. So, if you just got a document camera from a grant your principal wrote, zip to that chapter and figure out what in the world you can do with it. If you're studying geography and have heard that Google Earth is pretty neat, take a look at that chapter and start flying around the world. I tend to look at the dessert menu first when I go to a new restaurant, so I understand if you want to check out the options in the book before reading it straight through. Go right ahead!

I've also given you a Technology Continuum. I know that sounds serious, but it's simply a reflection tool. See where you stand on the Techie Continuum now, and then come back to it after you've been using this book for a while and try it again. I hope you'll find that you're well on your way to viewing yourself as a Techie Teacher. You may also want to use the Continuum to set your own personal goals and to encourage other educators to join you on the journey.

Relax. It's Painless!

By this point you may be thinking, "Yeah, this sounds good, but I don't have time." Boy can I relate to that. It's true. Lack of time and lack of training have kept schools from really using technology as a valuable learning tool over the years. Plair (2008) discussed technology fluency or integration as knowing when and how to use technology tools to enhance learning. Don't feel you must take on all 20 tools today. Instead take time with each one, determining when and how you would use the tool to enhance learning. Just reading this book shows your interest in spending some time learning new things.

I always suggest trying out new technology when you're relaxed, not the night before the principal's observation. I promise you if you try to learn something under pressure, it won't work and you'll crack under the stress. So, grab a cup of coffee, take a deep breath, and go step-by-step through the chapters you're most interested in. I really believe you will feel successful and energized. Your instruction will be enhanced and students will be engaged.

Technology Continuum

Read through the statements below. Select the one statement in each row that best describes you at this time. Keep track of your points to determine your current techie level.

1 POINT	2 POINTS	3 POINTS
I'm scared of technology. I'm afraid I'll break something.	I like technology, but I don't feel very confident.	I love technology and love to try out new things.
My idea of integrating technology is showing a video or writing on an overhead projector.	My idea of integrating technology is using digital media and websites to catch my students' interest.	My idea of integrating technology is seamlessly using technology tools throughout my instruction and having students use technology tools to show their understanding.
I'm not sure we need to use so much technology in our classrooms. Kids just want to be entertained.	I know I need to use more technology to engage my students, but I'm not sure how to do that. What do I do if it doesn't work?	I realize our students are digital natives and they want to be engaged with learning in a real way. Technology doesn't amaze them; they just expect it.
I've never used a web tool. What is that anyway?	I've tried a few fun web tools, but I'm not sure how that translates into the classroom.	I use web tools daily for instruction and as a way for students to create.
I feel overwhelmed with all of this new stuff, and the training at school was nonexistent or limited.	I'm uneasy because I haven't had time to play with the tools I have, and the training I received was limited.	I spend lots of time playing with new tools and have found they get easier to use the more I use the technology.
I've never used gadgets like document cameras or interactive whiteboards.	I've used some gadgets such as document cameras or interactive whiteboards, but I don't really know how to make the most of them.	I have gadgets such as an interactive whiteboard and document camera in my classroom, and I use them on a regular basis.

What's Your Techie Level?

If your total is 6–10, you're a Newbie Techie. You see technology and teaching as two separate worlds. This book can help you understand why technology can be a valuable teaching tool.

If your total is 10–14, you're a Techie on the Move. You believe that technology and teaching should go together, but you might not feel confident in your ability to implement new technology in your classroom. This book can help you enhance your skills and confidence.

If your total is 14–18, you're a Techie Teacher. You believe that it's all about the teaching, not the tools. That said, you strongly believe that technology tools enhance instruction and learning. This book should offer you new ways to expand on how you bring technology into the classroom.

Seeing Is Learning:
Web Tools That Enhance Teaching

When I think back through my own educational experiences, I realize how much things have changed. My memories of my elementary school classrooms are filled with walls of green chalkboards, an occasional bulletin board, and a few student-created decorations. Technology? What was that? The closest we came to having anything techie was the filmstrip machine—the one that beeped to tell you to turn to the next frame. I remember how we all tried to be on our best behavior so we might be chosen for the high honor of turning the filmstrip when that beep came.

Then there was the periodic rolling in of the double-reeled film projector. The films were actually wound on a metal wheel! We'd all pray that the wheel would be really big so the movie would be really long. I would cross my fingers, hoping my teacher could wrestle the film reel into place and make it work. It was so disappointing when the movie would get going and then the film would jump off the tracks and literally fly off the reel. Looking back, I bet my teachers hated those machines, but we loved them as students. They allowed us a look into another place or time. Watching those films broke up the monotony of the classroom, and their visuals seemed to stick with us forever.

Students today have probably never seen those old filmstrip and film reel machines. Instead, they can see videos being projected from the class computer to a big screen or an interactive whiteboard. They can watch movies on their smart phones. Flat-screen televisions connected to DVD players even take up residence in the classroom. No one's waiting for the beep or struggling with flying film. Do students still look forward to watching a film or video in the classroom? The answer is yes. The tools may have changed, but the need for visual representations of content and events is even greater.

Digital Natives Have Grown Up in a Very Visual World

From professional sports events with mega screens that constantly change to engage the audience, to churches where the pastor speaks and then shows movie clips to make a point on the big screen, our world is very visual. Think about the popularity of YouTube™. It has truly changed the way we share information. Yes, there are the silly videos of college students riding their bikes off rooftops, or the cross-eyed cat that sings, but there are also videos that teach us how to use the newest version of Word or PowerPoint or how to create a beautiful centerpiece for a special occasion. Pick a topic and you'll probably find a related video on YouTube™.

Here's an example of the power of visuals. My teenage daughter, Ashlyn, is a wonderful baker. She started baking at a young age and has become quite famous in her circles for the most delicious strawberry cake you have ever tasted. This is how serious she is about the baking thing: she makes her own birthday cakes. I know. It's so funny, but since no one else can do it as well as she can, she insists on this every year. A couple of years ago, she wanted to make a stacked cake covered in the colorful fondant you see on television. How hard could it be? First we went to the store and found a couple of books about how to create these amazing cakes. We purchased the needed supplies and headed home. After examining the books together, we were honestly still a bit lost as to how to make the cake. So, as any digital native would do, she headed to the computer and pulled up

YouTube™. We watched video after video of pastry chefs creating the type of cake she wanted to make. It didn't take very long until both of us felt confident enough to give it a go. She went on to create the most colorful and delightful birthday cake ever. The whole crowd was impressed with her skills. We give the credit to the how-to videos we watched online. When she hit a point of confusion, she would go watch one of the tutorials again.

This same thing happens every day in the lives of our students. They already understand how to use the Internet to find images and tutorials to help them understand the world around them. They may be searching for ways to improve their score on a video game, or they may be looking to see what the latest fashion trend is all about, but, either way, they're turning to visuals to help them learn.

Speak the Language of the Natives

Thanks to the Internet, you quite literally have at your fingertips a number of visual tools to help students learn new content or skills. Imagine building students' background knowledge about the setting of a book by creating a slideshow, or taking your students on a virtual fieldtrip to visit just about anywhere on Earth! Imagine the possibilities of a website that allows users to actually view today's front pages from more than 800 different newspapers in the U.S. and around the world.

This first section of the book provides you with resources to bring more visuals into your classroom. Here you'll learn how to use tools that create slideshows, videos, and graphic organizers. You'll learn how to access and use online instructional videos and interactive maps. But, as exciting as all of these can be, remember, they don't teach your students. You do. This section will also show you how to use these tools in meaningful ways to enhance your instruction as well as ways to hand these tools to your students so that they may share their learning in very visual ways. Seeing truly is learning in the 21st century.

Animoto

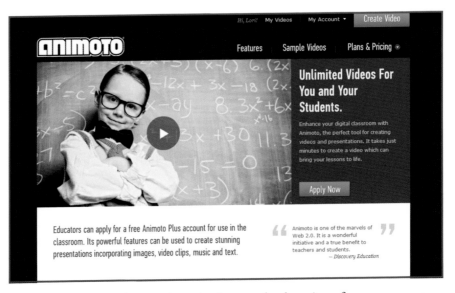

Educators can apply for a free Animoto Plus account for use in the classroom. Its powerful features can be used to create stunning presentations incorporating images, video clips, music and text.

Animoto is one of the marvels of Web 2.0. It is a wonderful initiative and a true benefit to teachers and students.
— *Discovery Education*

Picture this: A major earthquake just took place in a far away country. You want to use that current event to help your students learn about geography and the movement of the earth's plates. You realize that when you mention the country, however, most students won't have any idea where it's located or what it looks like. What's a teacher to do? How about quickly creating a slideshow featuring photos of that very country? You might even attach some appropriate music to help build an understanding of the culture. Now when you present the current event, students will have a basis for visualizing where it took place, and when the class discusses the impact of the earthquake, they'll have a connection to the people living there.

That's the power of slideshows or videos. They create visual frameworks. When students are able to build onto these visual frameworks, either by connecting the material presented to previously known concepts, or by building new ideas on top of them, learning takes place. There are many free or inexpensive online tools that enable you to create videos or slideshows. One of the easiest tools to use is Animoto.

Now What?

One great thing about Animoto is it offers educators a free subscription to the site; visit http://animoto.com/education/ to register. Animoto will take your application and review the information. If it appears you're truly an educator and you plan to use the site for educational purposes, you'll be granted a free subscription. If you'd rather not apply, you can use the free version of Animoto or pay the subscription fee of $30 a year, which allows you to make longer videos and gives you the ability to download your work. Follow this step-by-step process, and soon you'll have a customized video with a very professional look.

SELECT YOUR IMAGES

If you're already at a loss, wondering where you'll get the pictures, don't panic.

1. You can use pictures you've taken with your digital camera (or pictures you've scanned). To download images, plug your camera's cord or memory card into your computer.

2. Some cameras automatically place your pictures in a folder titled My Pictures. Other cameras prompt you to choose a folder in which to save the images. Check right now to make sure you know where that folder is located.

3. You can search for images online. Look for what are known as Creative Commons Images. These are images that are copyright-free, or free to use with a few restrictions.

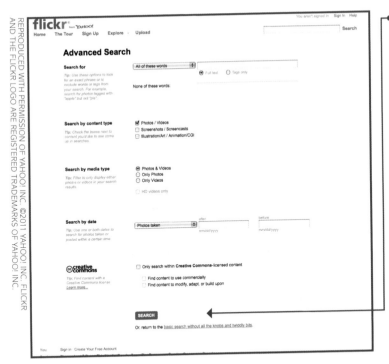

4. My favorite place to search for copyright-free images is on a site called Flickr at http://www.flickr.com/. Find the search bar and type in your topic. Now click on the Search button. When the next screen appears, click on the Advanced Search option and select Creative Commons, then click on the Search button again.

SAVE YOUR IMAGES

1. Once you find an image you like, be careful not to just copy the small image you see. That's called a *thumbnail,* and it won't really work very well.

2. To get the best quality picture, click once on the image to select it and then right click your mouse. (If you have a one-button mouse, hold down the control key and click.) You'll be able to view copyright restrictions and select a viewing size. You'll want to click on the largest available file size.

3. To save the picture, simply right click on the image and select Save Picture As. Assign the image a name and save it to your My Pictures folder or another folder of your choice. Continue searching for and saving images you want to use in your video.

CREATE YOUR VIDEO

Whew! Now that you've selected all of your images, you're ready to go!

1. Go to Animoto at http://animoto.com/ and log on. Click on Create Video, the blue button at the top of the screen.

2. You'll be prompted to choose your video style, which means you must select the type of background you'd like to use. These range from solid colors to holiday themes. Simply click on the one you like best.

3. Next you'll be asked to select the pictures you want to use in your presentation. Your options are to upload images from your computer, retrieve them from a website, or to select from images provided by Animoto.

4. Click on the Upload from Your Computer button. Find the folder where you saved your images and double click on it. To upload the image, click on the picture you want and then click the Open button.

5. You can also use video clips. Keep in mind the video clips should be quick snippets, not lengthy videos. The program won't use the entire video if it's over a few seconds long.

6. Once the pictures have uploaded, use the tools at the bottom of the page to spotlight, rotate, or duplicate your images. Click on the Add Text tool to key in a title and subtitle for your video. When you're finished, click on the Done button.

7. Next, choose the music you want to use. Animoto will suggest a selection for you to use. To accept it, click on Continue. To use another selection, click on Change Your Soundtrack.

9. Animoto provides a good selection of music for your video. To preview the music in their collection, click on the Select from Our Collection button. To use music saved on your computer as an MP3 file click on the Upload from Your Computer button.

10. At the Finalize Tab, you select how fast you want your images to move and make sure everything is the way you want it. When you're done, click on Continue.

11. You'll be asked to add any information you'd like included in your end-of-video credits. When you're done, click on Create Video.

12. The coolest thing about Animoto is that the website does all the work from here. Using the images you uploaded and the music you selected, Animoto creates a video with amazing transitions. The final product looks like it was done by a pro!

SHARE YOUR VIDEO

1. To share this outstanding video that you just created, click on the blue Share button under your video. You have many options.

2. You can post it directly to another site such as Facebook or Twitter by clicking on the appropriate icon. To send it via e-mail, click on the Email the Link button at the bottom of the screen.

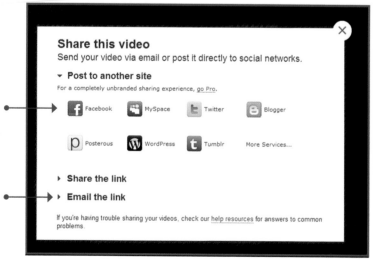

3. Click on the blue Embed button under your video and you will see the html code for it. If you have a website or blog, you can embed your video there. See page 134 to learn how to embed a video in a blog.

4. To download the video as an MP4 to save and share later, click on the blue Download button under your video.

Let Me Show You

LESSON Number Facts

Engage your students in number fact practice, and then feature their work in a math movie. They'll want to watch "their" movie again and again—what a great way to help them learn those important number facts!

1. Choose a number for which you want your students to learn the number facts. Let's say you chose 12.

2. Arrange students into small groups. Give each group a different set of 12 manipulatives. For example, you might give one group 12 Unifix cubes, another group 12 paper clips, another group 12 playing cards, and so on.

3. Ask members of each group to work together to set up their objects to show all of the different ways to make 12 using two parts. (For instance: 0 and 12, 1 and 11, 2 and 10, 3 and 9, and so on.)

4. As students work, circulate around the room taking pictures of each group's arrangements. It's not important to get a picture of every arrangement made by each group, but you'll want to have at least one photo for each way to make 12 using two parts.

5. After school, upload the photos to Animoto and create a slideshow, which you'll show to students the next day. They'll love seeing their work featured in a movie.

6. After watching the video, students should discuss all of the different ways to make the number 12 using two groups. Enlist the students to help you create a chart showing all of the possible combinations. Refer back to the video as necessary.

7. Don't forget to share the video with your students' families. Embed it in your classroom website or blog, or send home the website address in your newsletter.

Get Real

There are many other online sites that create slideshows and videos. Two of my favorites, which are also free, are Photo Peach at http://photopeach.com/ and Smilebox at http://www.smilebox.com/.

> I believe that the motion picture is destined to revolutionize our educational system and that in a few years it will supplant largely, if not entirely, the use of textbooks.
>
> —THOMAS EDISON (1922)

Do you wish you could select and upload more than one image at a time? You can! To do this, click on the first picture to select it. Now, find the next picture you want to use. Hold down the Control key and click on that picture. Notice how both pictures are now highlighted? That means you've selected them both. Continue holding down the Control key and selecting pictures until you've made all of your selections.

To select *all* of the pictures in your folder, click on the first picture in your folder. Now hold down the Shift key and click on the last picture in your folder. Voilà! You've just selected all of the pictures in your folder. What a time saver!

Tagxedo

You can make text come alive for students by stepping into the clouds—word clouds. Word clouds are visual representations of words, as shown in the illustration. The words can come from a passage of text. They can be key words in a unit of study. They can even be pulled from a website. The different shapes and colors within each word cloud can be used to highlight important ideas or focus on key concepts. You can use word clouds with any content area to introduce, review, or assess understanding.

One popular online word cloud tool is called Tagxedo (pronounced as tag-SEE-doh). The great thing about Tagxedo is that you don't need to register for an account or log in. You simply go to the site, add your own text, and let the tools create your word cloud. Tagxedo even allows you to make word clouds in actual shapes of objects (think cars or animals), or an image you provide. Ready to give it a try?

Now What?

Tagxedo is based on a Microsoft application called SilverLight. If you don't have it, don't worry. Tagxedo will prompt you to download it for free. If you're down-loading to your computer at school, you may need a technician to help you with this step because you probably don't have permission to download a program onto your computer. Once that's done, you're ready to proceed.

1. Go to Tagxedo at http://www.tagxedo.com/. Click on the blue Start Now button to begin.

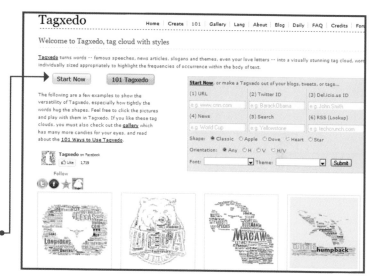

2. Take a look at the left-hand side of the screen. Under the heading Words, click on Load. You'll see three choices: You can browse your computer for a document already created; you can paste in the address of a website; or you can type in your own words.

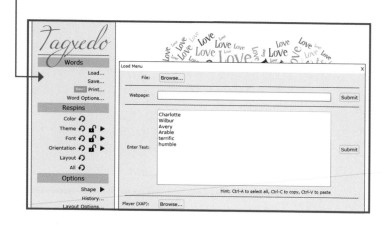

3. Try typing in some words. Here's a tip: The more times you type in a word, the larger it will appear in your finished word cloud. When you're done, click on Submit and the program will create a word cloud for you. Easy!

4. To change the color, font, or layout of your

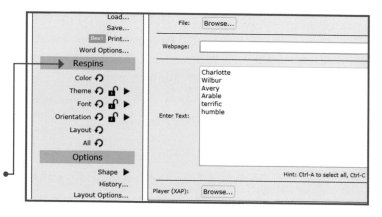

word cloud, look under the Respins heading. Click on the arrows next to each option to play with the format.

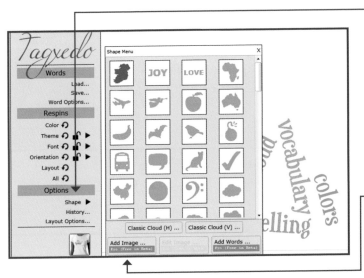

5. If you want your cloud to be in the shape of an actual object, look under the Options heading for the Shape feature. Click on the arrow next to the word Shape and then click on the shape you want to use.

6. To insert your own image, click on the Add Image button. Find the folder where you saved your image and double click on it. To upload the image, click on the picture you want and then click the Open button.

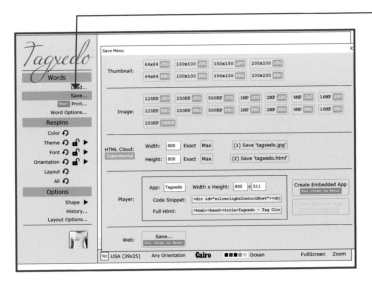

7. To save your word cloud, head back up to the Words heading and click on Save. Under the Image heading, choose the size jpeg file you'd like to use. A jpeg file means your creation is saved as a picture. The larger the jpeg size you choose, the better the printing quality.

8. You'll be prompted to name your word cloud

and select a folder to save it in. You're done! Now you can insert that picture into documents or presentations or post it online.

Let Me Show You

LESSON **1** Introducing Vocabulary

Use this organizer as the kick-off lesson for your next unit of study. It takes your K–W–L Chart to a whole new level.

1. Before class, create a word cloud that includes all of the key vocabulary words in your unit of study. Print out the word cloud and make a copy for each student.

2. Begin the lesson by projecting the word cloud for the class to see. (For options on how to do this, see pages 51 and 69.)

3. Hand out copies of the word cloud to students. Partner up the students and ask them to discuss the terms on the word cloud. Tell students to circle the words they know in one color and to use a different color to mark the unfamiliar words.

4. Bring the class back together to discuss the students' prior knowledge and concepts they still need to learn.

5. Ask students to refer to the word cloud throughout the unit. Have them make notes on their individual word clouds as they gain understanding of the terms.

6. Here's an optional step. Create a new word cloud featuring the words your students circled as unfamiliar. It's important to key in the words from each student's paper because the more times you type a word, the larger it will appear in the word cloud.

7. When you show students this new word cloud they'll be able to see which terms are the most unfamiliar to the whole class (those words will appear largest). At the end of the unit, show your students this word cloud again. Hopefully, all of the terms will be familiar to them now. It'll be a great way to show them how much they've learned.

LESSON **2** Community Building

Tagxedo can be an excellent tool for building a sense of community in a class. Use a computer lab or rotate students among computers available in the classroom.

1. Instruct each student to begin a Tagxedo by typing in his name and two or three adjectives that describe himself.

2. Next, ask students to rotate to the computer to their right. Once they are all seated, explain that their task is to add a word or two that describes the student who's the subject of the Tagxedo at their computer.

3. Writers also may choose to include character traits they appreciate in the person they're describing.

4. It's fine if different students type in some of the same words because when the word cloud is printed, those words will appear larger, indicating the attributes that are most recognized or appreciated.

5. Have students continue to rotate until every student has contributed to every Tagxedo.

6. Print the results and give each student his own personal Tagxedo. Now each student has a reminder of his importance in the classroom and of the traits his classmates appreciate.

LESSON **3** Self-Evaluation of Student Writing

Here's a great way to engage students in evaluating—and improving—their own writing.

1. Ask each student to select a piece of writing he'd like to analyze for overuse of a particular word or concept. Students will need to type their work into a document and save it as a text file. To save a document as a text file, students click on Save As and then select Text instead of Word.

2. Have students load their writing into Tagxedo.

3. Help them to discover that the size of each word in the cloud is based on how often it appears in the writing. If a student has overused a word, that word will be much larger than the others in the cloud.

4. Encourage students to edit their work accordingly.

Get Real

As you can imagine, this is the type of tool that could keep students busy for a long time, playing with shapes and colors. In fact, that's a potential problem. To keep things moving, make sure that before students create their word clouds they already have a plan. It's helpful for them to decide what words they want to use and even the shape they'd like to create. My policy is that before students create, they must show me their plan and I have to approve it. This prevents wasted time and poor content.

> Being literate no longer only involves being able to read and write. The literate of the 21st century must be able to download, upload, rip, burn, chat, save, blog, Skype, IM, and share.
>
> —MULLEN AND WEDWICK (2008)

If the object of the lesson is to illustrate a document, make sure to have the document saved in a folder that's easily accessible for students. Also, Tagxedo won't accept a document if it's been saved as a PDF or Word file. In order to insert a document into Tagxedo, you must save the document as a text file.

Tagxedo isn't the only word cloud maker. Wordle at http://www.wordle.net/ is also very popular. It doesn't provide the option to create shaped word clouds, but it's also free and simple to use.

YouTube™

Have you gone viral? No, I'm not asking if you've caught an infection. Viral is the term for online videos that have become hugely popular in a short amount of time. Sites such as YouTube™, Vimeo, School Tube, and Teacher Tube provide entertainment, information, and messages from amateur video creators. You can find just about anything you need to know by searching YouTube™. If you have a question about your computer or your favorite Hollywood celebrity, you can find videos to answer your questions.

YouTube™ limits the length of the videos posted, so the videos tend to provide rather quick and concise bits of information. Teachers can use these short videos at the beginning of instruction to hook students' attention, during a lesson to keep students interested, or at the end of the lesson to review the ideas presented and solidify the learning.

Now What?

Finding videos on You-Tube™ to use in your classroom works in much the same way you'd use any other search engine, such as Google.

1. Go to YouTube™ at http://www.youtube.com/. Find the search bar at the top of the screen, type in your question or topic, and click on the Search button.

2. Your task now is to look through the videos and find one that's appropriate for your content.

3. Once you've found the clip you want to use, you can add it to your favorites on your computer or insert it into your Live Binders online notebook (see page 123) so it'll be easy for you to find later when you want to show it to your students.

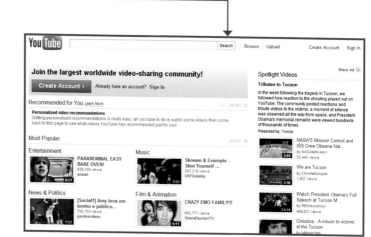

Let Me Show You

LESSON **1** Science Word Sorts

Here's a great way to introduce a new unit. Assess what students already know about the topic and then enhance their background knowledge with a video.

1. Prior to teaching the lesson, search YouTube™ (or another video site) for a video that introduces your science topic in an interesting way. Perhaps you're teaching a unit on life cycles, geology, or the solar system. Recently I was teaching a unit on the states of matter and found a fabulous video created by middle school students.

2. New videos appear on YouTube™ every day, so be sure to look often. Save the video to your favorites so you can easily find it again when you're ready to show it to your class.

3. Choose 12 to 15 words related to your topic. Write each word on an index card and place the cards in an envelope. You'll want to prepare one envelope for each group of students. Here's a look at the cards I used for my lesson on the states of matter:

molecules	ice	wood	soda
steam	fixed shape and volume	heat	carbonation
melt	atoms	takes the shape of container	no shape

4. Place students in small groups. Give each group an envelope. Ask them to sort their cards into categories that make sense to them. You don't need to give them the categories; their task is to discuss with their peers what they think the words might have in common.

5. Emphasize the importance of thinking about the *meaning* of the words. (I once had a group of students sort the words by spelling rules!)

6. As a whole class, discuss the findings of each group and talk about any areas of confusion.

7. Show the video you selected and then give each group time to look at their word sorts and, if necessary, rearrange their cards to reflect the information they learned from the video.

8. For closure, ask students to talk about what they learned by watching the video.

LESSON 2 Take a Brain Break

Provide brain breaks using your favorite videos to get students up and moving. Not only does it produce better learning, it models a healthy lifestyle.

1. Take time to search YouTube™ or your favorite video sites for dances like the Chicken Dance and the Macarena. The videos posted online for dance and music video games can be a great resource too. For example, *Just Dance* is a favorite Wii game, and you can find the dances online. (You won't need the gaming system to get students up and moving!)

2. Save the videos to your Favorites or create a Live Binder (see page 118) for Brain Breaks.

3. Use the dance videos during transitions between content areas. Use the videos when you see that glazed look in their eyes. Use the videos whenever your students need a brain break.

4. Get all the students up on their feet. Even if they don't do all the moves, they'll be up and ready to learn. This works really well because in just a few minutes you'll have regained their attention and energy. Your lesson will go much more smoothly after the brain break.

5. Do preview each video for appropriateness. Choose videos that are best for the age group you teach. Younger students will enjoy the Sesame Street characters and older students the gaming videos.

Get Real

So if YouTube™ is such a wonderful resource, then why do many school districts block its use? It's very common for school districts to block YouTube™ because of the potential for students to view inappropriate material. Some schools make it available to teachers, and others don't allow it at all. There are ways to deal with this issue.

> Today's young people . . . have learned to focus only on what interests them and on things that treat them as individuals rather than as part of a group or class. In an increasingly populated and crowded world, choice, differentiation, personalization, and individualization have become for today's young people, not only a reality, but a necessity.
>
> —MARC PRENSKY (2010)

First, let's look at the other free options available. Many schools that block YouTube™ do allow access to other video sites. School Tube, Teacher Tube, Watch Know, and Vimeo all offer videos that are similar to what you might have wanted to use from YouTube™. There are also paid subscription sites that provide quality videos. I like Discovery Education and Brain Pop. You can find the web addresses for each of these sites in the Appendix (see pages 174–76).

Another option is to download the video at home and bring it to the classroom to show. To save a video from the Internet you must have a tool to help you download it. One of the easiest video downloader sites I've used is Real Player at http://www.real.com/realplayer/.

Real Player is free and easy to download. It allows you to download videos from the Internet, edit videos, and share videos with others. Please understand that any time you download material you're dealing with copyright issues. Do not download videos that are copyrighted. Once you've downloaded the videos to your computer, you can then save them to a flash drive to take to your school.

Google Earth

Throughout my teaching career, I've always wanted to have the freedom and funding to take my students to places they've never been and see things they've never imagined. Unfortunately, the farthest we've ever been able to travel is to the local Nature Center or something similar. But things change, and technology makes the unthinkable doable. I may not be able to physically travel to exotic locations, but, using Google Earth, my students and I can take digital journeys all over the world.

Google Earth has changed the way we find directions and explore destinations. We're now able to "fly" to any place in the world, view the environment and buildings, and navigate our way to and from the location. When we're curious about where in the world Guam is, we head to Google Earth to show us the way. If we want to know where the newest school building for our town will be built, we look it up on Google Earth.

Now What?

To use Google Earth, you must first download the program from the Internet. It's free; it's easy; and it doesn't take long. To get started, visit http://www.google.com/earth/ and click on the Download Google Earth button. If you're downloading to your computer at school, it's likely that you'll need a technician to help you with this because you probably don't have permission to download a program onto your computer.

NAVIGATING THE SIDEBAR

1. Once Google Earth has been downloaded, it'll be listed in your programs or as an icon on the desktop. To begin, double click on the Google Earth icon. Take a look at the left-hand side of the screen; this is called the sidebar. You'll see three main categories: Search, Places, and Layers.

2. Under Search, you'll see Fly To and then a search box. Here you can type in the coordinates for a location, a specific address, or the name of a place. For example, you can type in your home address and find your street, or you can type in Eiffel Tower and fly to Paris.

3. After typing the location you want to visit, simply hit Enter or click on the icon of the Magnifying Glass to search. This will give you an aerial view of the location.

4. Now look carefully on the top right-hand side of the screen. You'll notice a white circle with the letter N (north). Roll over this image with your mouse, and you'll have access to some important navigation tools.

5. Click on these tools to look around, move, and zoom in and out of your location. Once you've zoomed in a bit on your location, the icon of a

Pegman will appear. Click and drag the Pegman to view your location from street level.

6. The next main heading on the sidebar is Places. This section keeps track of where you've been; and it also offers a list of places you may want to visit.

7. The last heading on the sidebar is Layers. Here you have a long list of options for how you may want to view a location. Perhaps you want to see buildings in 3D or view roads or photos others have embedded in the map.

8. Select the options you're interested in by clicking on the boxes. Please notice that within each main category there are even more selections. To see them, click on the plus sign by each item.

9. Be careful not to select too many layers because it can be very distracting to have all the layers open at once.

NAVIGATING THE TOOLBAR

1. You'll want to become familiar with the toolbar found across the top of the screen. Notice the yellow pin. That tool allows you to placemark a location. Click on the icon and then drag the Pin that appears on the screen to the place you want to mark.

2. You'll be prompted to name the location and provide information about it. Locations you placemark are saved to Places. Now you can quickly access this location by double clicking on the Pin icon.

3. Once you've placemarked a number of locations, you can create a tour that features them. After placing your pins on the screen, click on the Add a Path icon. Drag your mouse to connect the locations

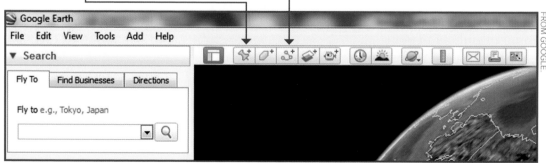

you want to visit. Label your tour in the pop-up window. Tours are saved to Places.

4. To record a tour that you can show again and again, click on the icon that looks like a video camera. A red recording button appears in the lower left of the screen. Click the red button to begin recording. Then move from location to location all the while recording your adventure.

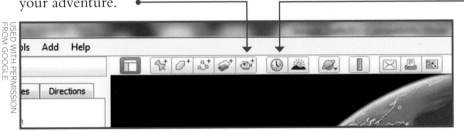

5. To see what a location looked like in the past, click on the Clock icon. A pop-up window appears with a timeline. Slide the bar on the timeline to select the time you'd like to view. If there are images of that location from that time period, you'll see the landscape change right before your eyes.

6. The Planet icon allows you to move to the sky, moon, or Mars. When you click on the icon, a drop-down menu appears. Click on the location you want to view.

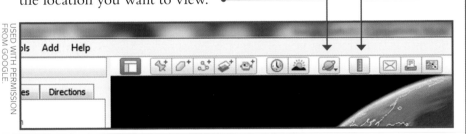

7. To calculate distance, click on the Ruler icon. Set the units of measurement you'd like to use in the pop-up window. When you roll over the map, your cursor appears as a box. Click on the location where you want to start measuring and then click on the point where you want to end your measurement.

There are definitely more advanced features of Google Earth, but this should get you and your students moving.

Let Me Show You

LESSON **1** Scavenger Hunt

Challenge your students to solve clues about historic places or important locations and then let them travel the globe to visit those locations. They'll learn the basics of Google Earth along the way too!

1. Before class, create a work sheet that provides students with clues about historic locations or important places. For example, if you're studying National Symbols, a clue might be "It stands by water and welcomes people to the United States."

2. You'll also want to create a note-taking sheet on which students can record their work. Look at the sample one included here for ideas. Make copies of both of these work sheets for the students.

Challenge	Location	Placemark Fact
1	New York Harbor	Statue of Liberty Gift from France and dedicated in 1886
2	Philadelphia, PA	Liberty Bell Chimed in 1776 for the first reading of the Declaration of Independence
3		
4		
5		

3. Model how to use the basic features of Google Earth. Zoom to a location and explore it. Be sure to show students how to add a place-mark to a location.

4. Once they are familiar with Google Earth, students work in pairs, if they're in the computer lab, or as a whole group if you have just one computer. Hand out the work sheets.

5. As students figure out each clue, they should fly to the location using the Search tool. Using tools under Layers, such as the National Geographic tool or the Travel and Tourism choice, students can learn new information, view videos or pictures, and learn interesting facts about each location.

6. Remind students to select just a few options in the Layers category so they won't be overwhelmed with information.

7. Instruct students to pin a placemark at each location. When naming each placemark, students should record a brief description of the location or an interesting fact they learned about the location in the description box on the computer and on their note-taking sheet.

8. If time allows, let students create a path and record a tour featuring all of their locations.

LESSON **2** Determine Mileage

At first look, it's evident that Google Earth is probably a favorite of Social Studies teachers, but it can be used to set the stage for any type of learning. In this lesson, math and literature come together as students use Google Earth to determine the total distance a book character has traveled.

1. Select a piece of literature in which the main character travels to multiple locations.

2. Ask students to use Google Earth to find each location to which the character traveled. Instruct students to insert a placemark at each location and then to create a path from place to place.

3. Show students how to use the ruler tool to measure the distance the character traveled from place to place.

4. Ask students to determine the total distance the character traveled. They'll be able to choose from a range of measurements, including centimeters, inches, yards, miles, even nautical miles.

Get Real

When you're using Google Earth with a whole group, have the locations already placemarked and the paths created ahead of time. This allows the instruction to progress more fluidly.

When Google Earth is being used by students to find locations or to create their own tours, make sure you have a set of directions or a graphic organizer for students to use during the process.

> Educators will need to move from the concept of building knowledge inventory in the minds of students to an approach that requires students to own their own learning processes and pursue learning, based on their needs of the moment.
>
> —WILL RICHARDSON (2008)

Also, make sure to let students know which options from the Layers category you want them to use and which ones they shouldn't use. It's very tempting to get off task and search for a friend's house or to click on zillions of layers that don't apply to the assignment.

There are so many truly amazing features of Google Earth. To help folks learn how to use them, Google Earth provides tutorials on the website. To view the tutorials, go to http://www.google.com/earth/. Find the blue band across the top of the screen and click on the Learn button. You can choose from Beginner or Advanced Tutorials.

Newseum

Newseum Blends High-Tech With Historical

The Newseum — a 250,000-square-foot museum of news — offers visitors an experience that blends five centuries of news history with up-to-the-second technology and hands-on exhibits.

The Newseum is located at the intersection of Pennsylvania Avenue and Sixth Street, N.W., Washington, D.C., on America's Main Street between the White House and the U.S. Capitol and adjacent to the Smithsonian museums on the National Mall. The exterior's unique architectural features include a 74-foot-high marble engraving of the First Amendment and an immense front wall of glass through which passers-by can watch the museum fulfill its mission of providing a forum where the media and the public can gain a better understanding of each other.

The Newseum features seven levels of galleries, theaters, retail spaces and visitor services. It offers a unique environment that takes museumgoers behind the scenes to experience how and why news is made.

Newseum atrium. (Maria Bryk)

"Visitors will come away with a better understanding of news and the important role it plays in all of our lives," said Senior Vice President Joe Urschel. "The new Newseum is educational, inspirational and a whole lot of fun."

When you watch television these days, do you ever feel overwhelmed with the amount of news being presented at one time? I started noticing this a few years ago. I must admit I enjoy watching entertainment news shows. I feel the need to keep up with the current trends in fashion and get the latest scoop on the celebrities. So, I'm watching the hosts banter back and forth about their weekend activities when all of a sudden breaking news of the latest tragedy in the Middle East and announcements by the president start zooming across the bottom of the screen. Then, before I know it, I look back up and the screen is split with multiple experts sharing their opinions about the appropriateness of wearing white after Labor Day. Good grief!

We're constantly bombarded with information—some valuable and some frivolous. It's hard to keep up. We definitely live in the information age, but how will students learn to sort through this hurricane of information? And, how do we know if the news we're getting is even-handed or accurate?

I would suggest teaching students how to read and compare information by using a helpful website called Newseum. Newseum is an actual interactive museum in Washington, DC. The museum and website were created to help the public appreciate and understand the news and media. The site provides many interesting features such as games and resources for teachers, but my favorite section is Today's Front Pages. Here, you and your students can actually view today's front pages from more than 800 different newspapers in the U.S. and around the world.

Now What?

The great thing about Newseum is that no log in or membership is necessary. Thanks to the generosity of the organization, we can share with our students the latest news by looking at front pages of newspapers.

1. Go to Newseum at http://www.newseum. org/. As you look at the homepage, scan over to the right-hand side of the screen and locate the Today's Front Pages button. Click on this button. You now have access to the front page of newspapers from just about anywhere.

2. To select a newspaper, simply click on its image. You can also access a newspaper by selecting it from a list or a map. You'll find these options near the top of the page in blue lettering. I like the map feature and so do my students.

3. Click on the Map button. You should see the map of the United States load on the left and the front page of a newspaper load on the right.

4. The screen shows just part of the map, but you can move the map around and view the rest of it or zoom in to a portion of it by using the navigational tools provided on the bottom left of the map.

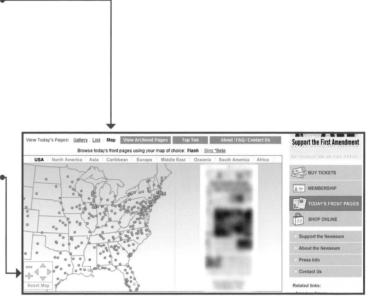

5. Scroll your mouse over the circles. Notice how the front page changes as you move over the circles. To see a newspaper in a larger view, find the appropriate location on the map and click on that circle. Another window will appear with a larger view of the newspaper.

6. You're not limited to viewing only newspapers from the United States. Look above the map. Do you see the names of the continents? Click on the appropriate one, and you'll get a choice of newspapers from that continent.

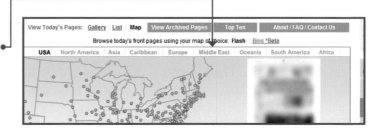

News-Leader, published in Springfield, MO USA   CLOSE X | Print Page | Readable PDF | Web Site

7. Select the newspaper you wish to read by clicking on the circle on the map. Now you can print it, view it as a readable PDF file, or, if you click on website, you can read the entire issue of the newspaper on the web.

Let Me Show You

LESSON 1 Critical Thinking

The Today's Front Pages feature from Newseum is a valuable tool because it allows students to view a current event from many different perspectives. In this lesson, students learn to compare and contrast information as well as recognize common themes or facts.

1. Plan to use this lesson on a day in which an important news event is either taking place or has just occurred the day before. Examples of this would be national elections, inaugurations, or natural disasters.

2. Prior to class, print out a sampling of front pages from newspapers around the country and the world. You'll need one newspaper page for each group of students.

3. To begin the lesson, ask students to share what they think they already know about the event. Discuss the geographic location of the event and what groups of people they think the event affects.

4. Show students the screen featuring Today's Front Pages. Scroll over the different locales and have students read the headlines on each of the front pages. If you have an interactive whiteboard (see page 51), have students come to the board and select the locations.

5. Have students discuss why they think the event is being mentioned in so many newspaper headings. Also ask them to discuss why some locations may not mention the event at all.

6. At this point in the lesson, place students in small groups and give each group a different newspaper's front page. Ask the students to carefully read, discuss, and take notes on the facts and details presented in their paper. Ask them to discuss what perspective they think their newspaper is taking.

7. Bring the class back together and have a conversation about the similarities and differences they found. Record their responses on a chart for all to see. Discuss the perspectives taken by the writers and the themes that appear throughout the different articles.

8. Help students to recognize that news can be presented in many ways and that they must compare resources and double-check facts instead of believing the first thing they see or read.

LESSON **2** What's Newsworthy and Why?

Comparing the front pages around the country or world helps students understand that what's important in one region of the country may not be important to other regions. The blizzard in the Northeast may not be nearly as important to Floridians as the predictions for tourism.

1. Follow the same procedures detailed in Lesson 1, but this time choose a day that's *not* particularly newsworthy on a national or international level.

2. To engage younger students in this critical thinking exercise, select only two front pages. Read aloud both pages and lead the whole class in a discussion.

Get Real

This is a pretty straightforward resource. It's important to recognize that because it shares front pages of real newspapers, however, there's no censoring. If students view the site on their own, they may see things you'd consider inappropriate for their age. Unfortunately, news isn't always pleasant and peaceful, so you may want to quickly browse through the front pages before the students get to work.

> Now that students are choosing to use the Internet as their personal medium, we are faced with the consequence of not teaching our children to decode the content. The growing persuasiveness of the Internet will lead to more and more students potentially being manipulated by the media.
>
> —ALAN NOVEMBER (2010)

Gadgets & Gizmos:
Using Today's Hottest Hardware

About eight years ago, I inherited my first SMART Board. I moved to a different grade level, and the new classroom had a SMART Board hanging on the wall. I received no training, no information, and no support for using this gadget. All I knew was that it was supposed to be great. Seriously, I didn't even know how to "turn it on"—I didn't know that the computer had to be on in order for the board to work. All I could figure out how to do was to pick up one of the colored pens on the tray and write notes on the board.

After a few weeks, my principal came down to see what I thought of the SMART Board. I told her I thought it was a very expensive purchase if all it could do was act as a whiteboard. I had no idea what an amazing resource I had in my room. Out of desperation I visited the room of another teacher who had a SMART Board and asked her to show me what it was supposed to do. Within a few minutes I was convinced of the possibilities. After I watched the teacher show me how the thing really worked, my teaching changed forever.

Maybe you're like me. Your district received some grant money or somehow budgeted to purchase some newfangled technology. Now you have the gadget or gizmo; the only problem is that you have little or no training in how to use it. The big question with technology for me is always, "So what?" Now that I have this thing, how will it improve my instruction and increase student achievement? It's important to go beyond just the basic functions of any gadget and to really dig into why this technology is helpful and how we can best use it with students.

You may be thinking, "I agree, but when or how am I ever going to figure out all this technology stuff?" Besides lack of ongoing training and support, typically the biggest obstacle to learning about a new gizmo or tool is *time*. That's right. The typical reaction I get from teachers is that "I don't have enough time to teach everything I need to teach and assess. I don't have enough time to just sit and play with a new tool. Now you want me to add technology to the long list of things I have to do? *When*?" Let's tackle these obstacles one step at a time.

Step One

Believe it or not, you don't have to become an expert with each tool or gadget. That's right. The truth is that this generation of learners probably knows more than we do about technology and is much quicker at figuring out the latest gadgets and gizmos. We're working with the digital natives. This is the first generation in which the students are essentially the experts at something, and we, as the adults, are the learners—the digital immigrants. So be willing to accept help from the natives. We have to change our mindset from thinking of ourselves as all-knowing to recognizing that we're learners ourselves. If your lesson doesn't go without a hitch, don't panic; just ask the students for suggestions and let them help. I have this theory. If you really want to know how to do something with technology, ask the natives! I've learned the most incredible tips and tricks by working in a partnership with students.

Step Two

Once you've let go of the anxiety about knowing everything, I suggest you do what I mentioned earlier: go visit someone who has experience with the device or tool you want to use. Go on your planning time. Or ask that teacher to teach your class and use the technology in the lesson. I've found that the best way for me to see the potential benefits of a tool and understand how to use it is simply to observe how someone else incorporates it in her teaching and how the students respond. If time is an issue, consider using Skype and a webcam (see page 97 to get started) to let all of your students sit in on that expert's class and benefit from his use of technology. The students can follow the same lesson as the other class, and you can get a lesson of your own.

Step Three

If you can't work out the observation time, head straight to your computer and dive into YouTube™. Yes, YouTube™. There are so many wonderful resources hiding amidst the videos of teenagers jumping off rooftops and babies eating their first birthday cakes. I'm serious. When I don't know how to do something, I go to You-Tube™ and type in the subject I'm curious about. Maybe I want to know how to set up a new document camera or how to take advantage of some new technique on my interactive whiteboard. When I type in my subject, I usually get a long list of videos. And I must say that I have laughed more than once about the fact that some genius eight year old taught me how to edit a video or make a podcast. Gotta love those natives! Seriously, look for tutorials online that show you step-by-step how to do things.

Don't limit yourself to YouTube™. Use your favorite search engine, such as Google. Type in the subject and add "tutorial" or "video" in the subject line. I think you'll be amazed at how much help is really out there. The wonderful thing about these tutorials is that you can view them over and over, stopping along the way to perform each step.

Step Four

The last suggestion I offer you for learning about a new gadget or gizmo is to simply . . . play. Now it's hard to play when you're stressed because you're trying to figure out the equipment for a lesson in an hour or the next day, so don't put that kind of pressure on yourself. If you decide you want to use this amazing interactive whiteboard you've never used before tomorrow, during back-to-school night, I'm going to tell you the truth: you're doomed to failure. Trying to learn something new under that kind of time pressure doesn't work for most of us, so instead make time to play when you're not up against a deadline.

Feeling better? Now that you're gaining confidence, let's take a look at the most popular gadgets and gizmos showing up in classrooms around the country.

SMART Board

Perhaps the hottest item right now in terms of technology equipment is the interactive whiteboard. Why all the hype? The purpose of an interactive whiteboard is to engage students by providing not only a visual tool, but also an interactive experience with content. During my years as a student, I learned pretty well by listening. If I could hear the teachers explain things— and then could chat about it—I learned. I didn't take many notes. I didn't draw pictures. I just needed to listen and talk. What's

interesting about this is that most people don't learn this way. I'm an auditory learner, and less than 10 percent of learners are auditory.

Think about this for a minute. How do most teachers teach? We talk, talk, talk. The problem is that less than 10 percent of our students are "getting" what we have to say. Clearly, the 80 to 90 percent of our students who are visual learners need to see the information. And the kinesthetic learners need to feel it. This is where tools like the interactive whiteboard come in. It effectively reaches all three types of learners. Visual learners can *see* what you're trying to explain; auditory learners can *hear* you as you explain it; and kinesthetic learners can *interact physically* with the board.

But there's more to it than just being able to reach our different types of learners. We have to reach them in a way that's meaningful to them as digital natives. Marc Prensky, the well-known technology advocate, believes that it's not that students can't pay attention to the old-fashioned way of teaching; it's that they *choose not* to pay attention to what we have to say (Prensky 2001). They're disengaged. You see, students are engaged in lots of things. They're playing video games. They're active in sports. They're writing and performing music. The problem is that when we try to share content using old methods that lack interactivity, they tune us out.

Thus, it's up to us to find ways to engage students so that they *want* to pay attention. And the best way to do that is to get them involved. We need to engage our digital natives with the interactivity that they love. The interactive whiteboard can help you do that in spades.

No longer do students need to simply sit and listen or stare at a stagnant image. With the interactive whiteboard, students can get up, move things around, interact with content, and learn in completely new ways. It's not that our curriculum and expectations have changed. All that's changed is the tool we're using to get those concepts across to our students. And it's a change for the better. Students are engaged as active participants in the learning process when they use the interactive whiteboard.

Now What?

The first thing to understand is that there are many brands of interactive whiteboards, just as there are many varieties of computers. For the sake of simplicity, I'm going to focus on SMART Boards. A SMART Board is the brand name of one interactive whiteboard, just as Kleenex is the brand name for one kind of tissue. Many folks call a tissue a Kleenex because of the brand's popularity and consumer recognition, and many folks refer to all interactive whiteboards as SMART Boards.

WHAT IS A SMART BOARD?

A SMART Board is a large interactive display board that's connected to a computer. You can physically move the text and images projected onto the board by just touching it. That's right! You don't need a mouse, and you don't have to be sitting at the computer. Any website or program that you call up on the computer can be projected onto the board. Then, with the touch of your hand, you can manipulate the objects and information you're projecting. Sound powerful? It is! Sound engaging for students? It's that, too!

To use a SMART Board you need four things: the board, a computer, a projector, and the special software that must be downloaded to your computer. SMART Boards operate with SMART Notebook software. The heart of the interactive whiteboard truly is that software. It includes interactive templates that help you create games that provide immediate feedback to students, as well as clip art, tools, and resources such as rulers and maps.

Here are just a few of the things you can do with your SMART Board.

WHAT YOU CAN DO WITH A SMART BOARD	HOW THIS FEATURE COULD BE USEFUL IN YOUR CLASSROOM
Write or type	Check an anticipation guide after reading a story
Move manipulatives around	Provide students skills practice in counting money or measuring objects
Hide information until you are ready to reveal it	Reveal a poem a little at a time so students can analyze each phrase
Create a spotlight	Enlarge a location on the map so students can clearly see it
Record a lesson	Capture your entire lesson including the images on the board and your voice and create a movie for students to review again and again

SMART Boards offer all sorts of tools to help your students learn. The good news is that you don't have to have mastered *all* of those tools in order to get started. You can begin gradually and add more to your "repertoire" as your comfort level and your confidence increase. Here's what I'd recommend.

STEP ONE

To become familiar with the SMART Board, find lessons that have been created for the SMART Board by other teachers who use one. To do that, go to SMART Exchange at http://exchange.smarttech. com/. The lessons are free to download and use. Once you download a lesson to your computer, you can use it with your SMART Board. Not only will you look like an expert, but you'll also begin to understand how to use your board.

It may seem strange that I'm not starting with a discussion of each tool on the toolbar of your SMART Board, but from my experience, until you really understand what a great lesson using the board looks like and feels like, knowing all the tools in the world won't translate into strong instruction. Instead, I've found that once you see examples of the tools in action, you'll be able to understand how and why things like writing in rainbow ink or zooming in can be integral to instruction and not simply cool features.

STEP TWO

Learn a few of the basic SMART Board tools—just enough to let you take advantage of the board's capabilities and get beyond using it as a projection screen. You're not looking for the fanciest tools available; you want the ones that will have the most immediate impact on your instruction.

Here's the "starter kit" I'd recommend. Look at your toolbar and find the following "must haves."

TOOL	WHAT IT LOOKS LIKE/LOCATION	WHY WOULD I USE IT?
Write	It looks like a pen. Find it on the toolbar.	To write letters, words, numbers
Type	It looks like a capital A with a red line underneath. Find it on the toolbar.	To type letters, words, numbers
Gallery Essentials	On the side of your SMART Notebook page, click on the second tab (the one with a landscape portrait) and then open Gallery Essentials.	To find images, grid paper, handwriting paper, manipulatives, etc. to use with students
Lesson Activity Toolkit	On the side of your SMART Notebook page, click on the second tab (the one with a landscape portrait) and then open the Lesson Activity Toolkit.	To create interactive games and activities that provide immediate feedback when played or used
Add a New Page to the Document	It looks like a piece of paper with a tiny green circle with a white plus sign on it. Find it on the left-hand side of the toolbar. You can also find it below the tabs at the bottom of the page.	To add pages so that instruction flows and you have room to add to your already prepared pages
Attachment	It looks like a paperclip. It's the third tab on the side of your SMART Notebook page.	To attach documents, SMART Notebook lessons, websites, PowerPoint presentations, and other resources right to your lesson

STEP THREE

Now you're ready to start planning your own interactive whiteboard lessons. A quality interactive whiteboard lesson should be more than one quick activity for the students to see or do. It should start with an interesting introduction and build to the lesson's conclusion. Along the way, students should receive small bits of information followed by opportunities to immediately check their understanding. This process allows you to constantly assess and redirect your instruction as needed. And, please, make sure the students are up at the board more than you are. That's right! It's called an interactive whiteboard because its purpose is to help students interact with the content.

Let Me Show You

LESSON 1 Parts of Speech

Students will learn about the basic parts of speech by using visuals and interactive templates on the SMART Board.

1. Before class, find a picture of a person per-forming an action, such as riding a bike, by look-ing in the Gallery of your SMART Notebook Lesson Activity Toolkit. I found one by typing "bicycle" in the Gal-lery search bar. This will be the first page of your lesson.

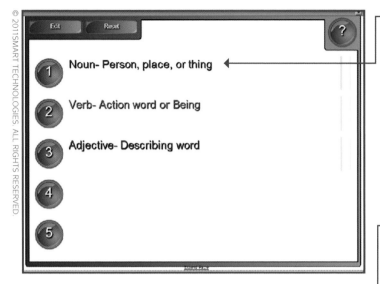

2. Use the Note Reveal template from your Lesson Activity Toolkit. This allows you to input information that can be revealed to students as they click on it. Create a page that defines nouns, verbs, and adjectives. This is page 2 of your lesson.

Noun	Verb	Adjective
boy	rides	blue (hat)

3. Prepare a chart with the following headers: Noun, Verb, and Adjective. Use the Table Creation tool on the toolbar. It looks like a calendar. This is page 3 of the lesson. Students will fill in the chart by referring back to the information found on page 1.

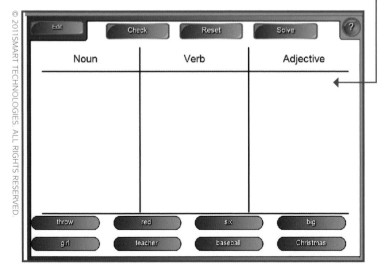

4. Use the Category Sort template from the Lesson Activity Toolkit to create a page where students sort words by dragging and dropping them into categories. You may also want to try the Vortex template for categorizing. Students love that template! This is the final page of your lesson.

5. To begin the lesson, introduce the concepts of noun, verb, and adjective. Project the image of the person riding the bike and ask students to describe what they see as it relates to the parts of speech.

6. Invite students to come up to the SMART Board and circle or draw arrows to highlight their observations.

7. Reveal to students the definitions of the parts of speech that you created on page 2 of your lesson.

8. Flip back to the illustration on page 1 of your lesson so students can refer to their observations. Have them use the information from that page to complete the chart you have placed on page 3.

9. Check student understanding by having them drag and drop words into the different parts-of-speech categories.

10. Based on student responses, you'll either reteach or move on to the next set of skills.

LESSON 2 Do the Math

Use SMART Board tools to provide students with practice counting money.

1. Prior to the lesson, locate a video online (see page 29) that demonstrates the math concept you're teaching. For example, if you're teaching how to count money, head to Teacher Tube at http://www1.teachertube.com/ or Brain Pop at http://www.brainpop.com/ to find a video that teaches about money in a fun way. Brain Pop is a subscription site, but it has some free videos available so it's worth your time to check it out.

2. Use a template like Pairs or Tiles from the SMART Notebook Lesson Activity Toolkit to construct a game about counting coins. You'll want to use this at the end of the lesson to check for student understanding.

3. Perhaps you'll also create a page where students must drag coins or bills into a piggy bank or have students match price tags with the correct combination of bills and coins to practice the skill.

4. Begin the lesson by playing the video on the SMART Board. Ask students to talk with a partner about what they noticed.

5. Drag over the coin manipulatives from the Gallery. Introduce the coins. Instead of dragging over many of the same coin, use the Infinite Cloner option on the drop-down menu that appears when you click on the coin. You'll see a little arrow in the corner. Click on that arrow and choose Infinite Cloner. Now when students drag a coin, the original one stays in place and you have others for students to use. Such a handy feature, that infinite cloner! Have students come to the board to manipulate the coins and practice counting.

6. After completing several example problems, pass out actual coin manipulatives for students to use at their seats. That way, as one student is at the board working, everyone else has the opportunity to practice the skill too.

7. Invite students to play the game you constructed. After assessing their performance, you'll decide to either continue practicing the skill or move on to more complicated problems.

Get Real

Having an interactive whiteboard provides motivation for learning new content and reviewing things already learned. There's a problem, however, when only one person can be at the board at a time. So what do all the other students do while a classmate is at the whiteboard?

Location is key. If the class is playing a game or you want to involve multiple students in the lesson, make sure that students are sitting close to the board, ready to go. For games, you may consider lining up students in two teams facing the board; each student is prepared and waiting to take his turn. When he finishes, he moves to the back of the line. Not only does this help with classroom management, it gets students on their feet—something that's always healthy and good for the brain.

When only one student is at the board, make sure to use cooperative learning strategies with the rest of the

> Interactive whiteboards have great potential [to] improve student achievement. However, simply assuming that using this or any other technological tool can automatically enhance student achievement would be a mistake. As is the case with all powerful tools, teachers must use interactive whiteboards thoughtfully, in accordance with what we know about good classroom practice.
>
> —ROBERT MARZANO (2009)

class. You might ask each student to talk to her shoulder partner about the topic, or to tell her partner what she would select if she were at the board. Graphic organizers, note-taking sheets, dry-erase boards, and manipulatives can help keep students focused on the task. If the lesson requires that students move letter tiles around on the interactive board, make sure the other students have letter tiles to work with at their desks too.

Perhaps you have a different brand of interactive whiteboard in your classroom. Here's a chart to help you locate lessons created specifically for your brand of whiteboard.

TYPE OF BOARD	TEACHER RESOURCES	WEBSITE
Promethean/ActivBoards	Promethean Planet	http://prometheanplanet.com/
eInstruction/Interwrite Boards	eI Community	https://www.eicommunity.com/
Mimio	Mimio Connect	http://mimioconnect.com/

iPad

iPads are some of the newest of the technology gadgets sweeping our homes and classrooms. An iPad is considered a personal mobile device. It isn't a computer, but it does allow you to surf the web and read and write e-mail messages. The reason the iPads are so attractive to users is because of the literally thousands of apps available. An app is a software application that allows you to do something. If you have a need, someone has or will create an app to help you accomplish your task. There are apps for managing your day, counting your calories, reading books, and playing lots of games.

I love my iPad. I've loaded it with apps for everything I need to keep my life organized. It's light and easy to carry around, and it doesn't need a mouse or keyboard. It allows me to play my favorite songs, view podcasts, watch the episode of *Big Bang Theory* I missed last week, and beat my own personal best on Angry Birds. I can even use it to browse the U.S. National Archives, explore the fossil collection at the American Museum of Natural History, and send out parent conference sign-up invitations.

Are you wondering if this neat gizmo has a place in your classroom? You aren't alone. School administrators and teachers are considering using iPads in the classroom as an alternative to purchasing a class set of computers or mobile laptop carts. Even though iPads are very new, many risk takers have decided to give them a go. Some schools are purchasing them to assist teachers with their tasks, and others are providing class sets for students to access throughout the day.

Ponder the Possibilities

Novelty can certainly play a role in engaging learners. We all like something different to change it up. iPads are different from computers and interactive whiteboards, yet they do provide interactivity and constant feedback. Our students tend to be visual and kinesthetic learners. With the iPad, they can clearly see the book, video, or game and touch their way to understanding.

An idea that's attracting much buzz from educators is the possibility of using iPads to replace traditional textbooks and reading materials. Purchasing textbooks and encyclopedias is very costly, and books take up a lot of space in the classroom. Many would also argue that it's unhealthy for kids to be tromping around with 50 pounds of weight in their backpacks. Thousands of books from picture books, to novels, to the newest social studies textbooks are now available to download from the Internet to the iPad using iBook, another app. Once a book is on the iPad, students can use other apps to take notes on the pages, add virtual sticky notes for reminders in the text, and highlight digitally.

Believe it or not, games are a big reason for using iPads with students. I'm not talking about the frivolous games of our youth like Candy Land or Mouse Trap, although many would argue their educational value. What we want to examine is the level of gaming our students have grown up with. Video games, which for many years had been given a bad rap, actually engage us. When the strategy of the game is complex and the visuals are appealing, players will stick with the game until they figure it out. I cannot say the same for a game of Monopoly. It doesn't quite have the same staying power. The reason gaming, meaning digital games, is so popular is because the games are challenging and often require collaboration with others, as well as problem-solving.

This is a generation that sees learning as playing, and they want the playing to be challenging. The iPad apps provide us with games that can serve as learning tools. Of course, there are some, like Candy

Land, that are just for kicks, but there are apps that really make students think and help them to learn new concepts by engaging them in what they know best—games.

Devise a Plan of Action

Before you run out to buy a class set of iPads, you need to know why and how you'll use them. Your purpose must be clear. If you don't have a plan for instruction and learning, they'll end up sitting unused because you don't have a focus. Let's consider how many iPads might work for your situation. You may only want one right now, just for yourself so that you can get your work accomplished. You may be interested in enough for every group of three to four students to share. Maybe you feel that a one-to-one iPad implementation is necessary, with each student using one of her own.

How will you use the iPads with students? Will they be primarily used for reading books or searching the web? Will students use content apps to play their way to learning? Will you have organizational apps on the iPads to help with note taking and classroom assignments? Maybe you have limited funding for your music, science, or design class and using the apps is most cost effective? For example, if your school doesn't have funds for the entire 8th grade to dissect frogs this year, there's a Frog Dissection app that takes students through a virtual dissection. Or perhaps your school lost its music teacher due to budget cuts, and now you have to teach music in your elementary classroom. There are apps to help you teach about the types of music, instruments, singing on pitch, and even the basics of music composition.

Really think through the whole idea. For instance, if you were to get several iPads or an entire class set, where would you store them? You'll need a cabinet or shelving to safely and securely store the iPads, as well as a place where all of them can be charged every day or two. Look around your room. Where are the outlets? Do you have enough juice to get them all going?

Realistically, cases and screen covers should be a part of the total iPad purchase. As cool as the iPad looks, if you drop one without a case or screen cover, you're going to end up with broken glass everywhere and a huge loss of investment. Plan to purchase at least covers for each of the iPads you want to use with students.

You'll also need to consider your access to iTunes and the possible cost involved with purchasing apps for your classroom. Do you have funding to purchase educational apps if they aren't available for free?

And finally, do you have Wi-Fi capability? The beauty of the iPad is that it's wireless. If you're going to purchase a set of iPads, make sure your district will support you by providing a router for Wi-Fi capability in your classroom. Some buildings have gone wireless throughout, but for a very reasonable cost ($50 to $100), you can connect a router that will permit Wi-Fi in your classroom.

Do the Math

Now let's do a little calculating and figure out the options for purchasing these neato devices. As of this writing, the iPad starts at less than $500; more powerful versions currently cost more than $800, though many predict that those prices will come down in the future. The devices at the lower end of the price range have 16 GB of memory and Wi-Fi access. The higher end model has much more memory and 3G technology, which allows you to access the web and your apps without Wi-Fi. Of course, there's a cost for that feature. You have to purchase what's called a data plan from a network service provider. With the data plan you basically pay for the use of the Internet. For most schools, the way to go is the basic iPad with Wi-Fi access (no need to tack on that extra cost). Once you have your plan of action in hand, start writing those grants and petitioning your administrators for support.

Now What?

Let's start at the top. The first thing you'll want to do is to make sure iTunes is loaded on your classroom computer because that's where you'll be managing your iPads. You need iTunes because that's where you'll go to purchase apps, podcasts, music, etc. When you load iTunes, you'll also set up a password and username, which allows you to purchase items. To download iTunes, go to http://www.apple.com/itunes/. You may need a technician to help you with this because you probably don't have permission to download a program onto your school computer.

GO SHOPPING!

1. Once iTunes is downloaded, it'll be listed in your programs or as an icon on the desktop. When you need it, you'll just double click on that icon.

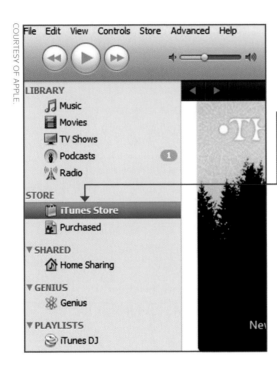

COURTESY OF APPLE.

2. Look to the left of your iTunes screen and find the icon that looks like a shopping bag. Click on it to go to the iTunes Store.

3. Look across the top of the screen until you find Apps. Click on Apps. Here you can search for any topic you'd like. Type the subject you want in the search bar.

4. For example, if I need to help my high school students understand cells, I type in "3D cell." I find a free app that takes students into cell construction, uses video, and allows students to explore the various parts of the cell. Jackpot!

5. Once you find an app you're interested in, you can get more information about it by clicking on its title. To "purchase" the app (even if it's free), you must click on Buy. The app will be loaded to your iTunes account.

6. A pop-up window will ask you for your password and to verify the purchase. So, if you happen to click on something that you don't want, don't worry. You have to okay the purchase before you're charged.

7. Wasn't that fun? You got to go shopping, and you found tools to engage your students—what a great resource!

LOAD YOUR IPAD

1. So now you have apps, and maybe even music and podcasts in your iTunes account. To see what's in your iTunes account, look on the left-hand part of the screen. Click on the different categories to see what you've loaded.

2. Click on each app (and any other media) you want loaded to the iPads.

3. Plug an iPad into your computer using the cord provided. Immediately a message will appear on your screen to tell you that the iPad is syncing with your iTunes and not to unplug.

4. All of the items you selected from your iTunes account are being loaded onto the iPad.

5. You'll need to do this with each iPad. When the process is complete, a window will appear with a message to tell you that the download is finished, and you can now safely disconnect the iPad from your computer.

COURTESY OF APPLE.

YOU'RE READY TO GO

1. To turn on the iPad, push the button on the front of it. The screen will turn on. Look to the top right-hand corner for the icon of a battery. This shows you how much charge you have.

2. Make sure your iPads have been plugged into the wall or the computer and have charged completely before handing them out to students.

3. If you're holding the iPad vertically and turn it horizontally, the screen orientation will automatically change. I like a bigger onscreen keyboard, so I turn my iPad in a horizontal direction.

4. To choose an app, all you have to do is touch it. Instead of a mouse, you use your finger to operate all the tools. An onscreen keyboard pops up when you need to type or use keyboard tools.

5. When you want to get back to the original screen with all the app choices, push the button on the front of the iPad again and you'll get back to the original screen.

6. If you leave the iPad sitting idle, eventually the screen will fade. You can push the tiny black button on the top of the iPad to turn off the screen.

Let Me Show You

LESSON Poll the Audience

Get students involved in your lesson—and get instant formative assessments too—by using the eClicker app. Students can cast their votes using their iPads.

1. This is a great app to use with any age group or content area. Go to the iTunes store and search for eClicker. You'll find that they have both the eClicker Host and the eClicker. The Host costs $9.99. You'll need it in order to type in your polling or review questions. The student app, eClicker, is free.

2. Download the Host app to your iPad and the free version to the students' iPads. When you connect to the Wi-Fi network in your classroom, the Host version will provide you with the website address your students will need in order to access the polling feature. Students can type this address into the Internet address bar on their iPads, or if you link the address to your class website or blog, they can just click on the link from there.

3. You'll find that questions already exist in the Questions tab for you to use, but you can also create your own. To enter a question, click on the + sign on the Questions tab and then type your question in the box provided. You can choose how you want students to answer each question. Multiple choice, true/false, and fill in the blank are some options to try. You can create an entire Questions set and then save it to use with your class.

4. To begin a session using the eClicker app, ask students to open the website address. Now you can ask them a question and they can click on their answers. You can ask the questions all at once or just a few at a time in random order throughout a lesson. The Host eClicker provides you with immediate feedback. It lets you know how many students answered correctly and who answered what.

5. Now you can make your lesson about the history of your state or who said what in *Romeo and Juliet* interactive and meaningful. With eClicker, you're not only able to give students immediate feedback for their thoughts, but based on the data you receive after asking each question, you can change your instruction to meet their specific strengths and weaknesses. Talk about a tool that helps you with diagnostic teaching!

Get Real

The iPad certainly encourages greater student engagement than the typical textbook. However, iPads are among the newest forms of technology entering classrooms today. This means we have not perfected their use quite yet. It will take a lot of trial and error to see how this interesting tool will be most effective.

Effective classroom management is needed in order to keep students safe and keep the equipment in good shape. Screen covers and iPad cases are necessary to protect the iPads. Because of the glass screens, students need to be careful not to drop them. Also, you need to constantly monitor use to help keep students on task.

> One of the biggest challenges educators face right now is figuring out how to help students create, navigate, and grow the powerful, individualized networks of learning that bloom on the Web and helping them do this effectively, ethically, and safely.
>
> —WILL RICHARDSON (2008)

Just as you take time to find quality websites, it's necessary to spend time looking for quality apps. It's helpful to network with other teachers and share the treasures you discover. Here are some of my favorite apps available on iTunes: Magic Piano, Dropbox, Toontastic, American Museum of Natural History, and National Archives–Today's Document. To find these apps, just enter each name into the search bar on iTunes.

Document Camera

When I ask teachers what type of gadgets or gizmos they'd really like to have in their classrooms, someone always says, "I want an Elmo." Now we aren't talking about the cute, furry critter on Sesame Street. We're talking about one of the most popular brands of document cameras. In fact, most teachers would take just about any brand of document camera. Why? Because with a document camera you can place any book, piece of student work, photograph, manipulative, even a tiny snail scooting along underneath its lens, and the image of that object is projected live and in person for all to see. There are no overhead transparencies to make. Just place the item you want students to look at under the document camera and start teaching.

The document camera not only replaces an overhead projector, it steps things up quite a bit. Most document cameras also allow you to capture video or still pictures of the object placed under the camera. This can be really helpful when reviewing lessons. Imagine doing a science experiment with your first graders about the life cycle of the frog. You use your document camera to show actual tadpoles swimming around and you observe their tails. Each day you take a photo or video of the tadpoles until you have new frogs living in your classroom. Getting up close and personal with the tadpoles is cool in itself, but then having a record of each day's observations makes the learning even more powerful.

Document cameras can be used in hundreds of ways in the classroom. For math lessons, students can place the coins or pattern blocks under the lamp and manipulate them. Science concepts, such as identifying types of rocks, can be enhanced by using the camera.

Even labeling the states and capitals can seem like fun when the map is seen in wide view. Document cameras can be a great alternative if you don't have an interactive whiteboard, or they can be used right along with your interactive whiteboard.

Document cameras range in cost from $200 to $2,000. They are very popular items for grants because of the relatively low cost. Many different companies make document cameras. A few of the most popular manufacturers are Elmo, Lumens, SMART, AverMedia, Samsung, and Ken-A-Vision.

Now What?

Most document cameras require an LCD projector, a computer, VGA cables (these are the type of cables that link computers and LCD projectors), and the software that accompanies the document camera. In general, the set up is really very simple.

1. Install the software that accompanied your document camera onto your computer. It's helpful to set up your document camera close to your computer. That way you can easily access the software, which usually includes the video recording and picture-taking features.

2. Most document cameras either plug directly into a projector, or they connect to a computer that's connected to a projector. You'll either use your VGA cable to connect your document camera straight into the projector or to a computer already connected to the projector.

3. A few of the newer document cameras are actually wireless, which is a pretty neat feature. That way, you don't have to be tied to one place in the room right by your computer.

4. Now it's showtime. Turn on your projector, document camera, and computer (or turn on the projector and document camera if you went directly through the projector). Place your item under the lamp on the camera and begin teaching.

5. Some document cameras actually have a base on which you place your items under the lamp. This may be referred to as the workspace.

6. Consider projecting your images onto either your dry-erase whiteboard or your interactive whiteboard to allow students to work with the projected images.

7. If you're projecting correct letter formation for handwriting, students can practice the letters by writing on the interactive whiteboard or the dry-erase whiteboard under your example.

Let Me Show You

LESSON 1 Writing

Use the document camera to spotlight your authors and their work. It'll get students motivated to share their writing!

1. Select a passage from a favorite book that models an important writing skill you want your students to focus on in their own writing. For instance, you might decide to choose a passage that models sentence structure, voice, descriptive language, or colorful language.

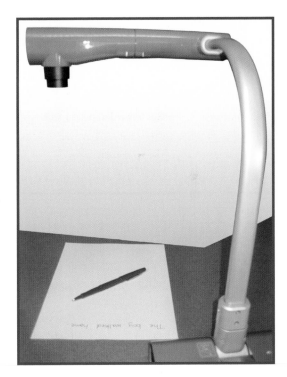

2. Place the book under the document camera and read aloud the passage you selected. Ask students to examine the writing for the skill you're teaching.

3. Let's say you're focusing on descriptive language. Invite students to come up to the document camera and point out the action verbs in the passage. If you're projecting onto a whiteboard, let students go to the board and circle the verbs.

4. Discuss the power of using more descriptive verbs when writing.

5. Write a few sentences or a paragraph using verbs such as "go," "said," and "ran" on a piece of paper under the document camera. Ask students to help you spice up the verbs by using words such as "traveled," "exclaimed," and "zipped," much as the author did in the writing sample you shared.

6. Have students move to their seats, get out their writing notebooks, and begin their own writing. Confer with students as they write and then move around the room to check on everyone's progress.

7. During Author's Chair or share time, have a few students share their writing using the document camera. Encourage the other students to give positive feedback.

8. Watch as the excitement grows. Students love to see their work projected! Now everyone wants to do great writing so their work will be shown. Make sure to include all levels of writing so no one feels their work is not appreciated.

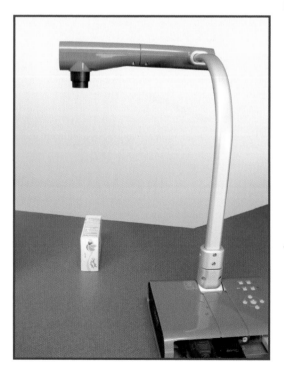

LESSON 2 Food Labels

Help students understand how to read nutrition labels and make healthy food choices.

1. Before class, you'll need to gather a collection of food packages from both healthy and unhealthy foods.

2. Have students brainstorm the differences between healthy and unhealthy foods. Use the document camera to project images of healthy food choices and junk food. Discuss what makes a food healthy.

3. Show students the nutrition label on the back or side of a package of food. Discuss how to read the label. Focus on fat, carbohydrates, and protein amounts.

Also, explain how to read the list of ingredients to see if something is healthy.

4. Have students take turns selecting a food package. Before the student places the label under the document camera, ask the class to guess if the food is healthy or unhealthy and if it's high in fat, calories, sodium, and so on.

5. Have the student place the package under the lamp and read the label to find out if it's healthy or unhealthy.

Get Real

Something you'll want to check out before purchasing a document camera is the clarity of the image. Look for resolution, the type of light the camera uses, and the zooming capacity. The higher the resolution, the sharper the image will be. Also, check the features of the document camera. Does it record video, take pictures, work with other software you might have, such as your interactive whiteboard software?

Consider your setup. Place your document camera in a spot that you and your students can easily access. If it's covered up at the end of your desk, you aren't very apt to use it. Try placing it on an empty table or desk close to your computer. Make sure there's plenty of room to place your items under the camera's lamp. You don't want to hear the crash of something getting knocked off an unsteady surface! Finally, keep the path to the camera clear. You don't want anyone tripping over cords.

Visual rules to remember:
- The brain pays attention to color.
- The brain pays attention to size.
- The brain pays attention to orientation.
- The brain pays attention to movement.

—MARILEE SPRENGER (2010)

If you're looking for a cheaper way to go, consider using a webcam as a document camera. Look for one such as the HUE webcam by Clique. It has a moveable neck so it's easy to manipulate and project images. As I write this, the HUE can be purchased for less than $50 from Amazon at http://www.amazon.com/. In times of budget crunches, such as many schools are facing today, the webcam is a great alternative.

Digital Video Cameras

Do you remember watching old family movies as a kid? Can you believe Mom could tease her hair that high? And check out those plaid pants on Dad! Okay, the footage seemed a little choppy, and maybe there wasn't any audio, but those movies had personality. They captured a moment in time, and that's what makes them special. The desire to "capture the moment" is nothing new, but luckily for us, the technology sure is.

Long gone are those intimidating days of hauling out the enormous video recorder and tripod from the school library. Remember praying you wouldn't drop the camera as you tried screwing it onto the tripod? Then there were all of those buttons. Good grief! All you wanted to do was film your class acting out their play. And finally, there was that strange-looking disc or tiny cassette the movie was captured on. How were you going to show *that*? Was all that work for nothing?

Video cameras have changed drastically over the years. Not only are the visual and audio quality much better, but today's cameras are also so much simpler to use. Best of all, they allow you to view and share videos in ways that were unimaginable only a decade ago.

Today's digital video cameras provide you the opportunity to share your videos with the world almost immediately.

Imagine this scenario. You want to film your students acting out *Henny Penny*. You get out your digital video camera. It fits in your hand. There are no cords, no memory card, no weird cassettes or discs. You simply aim the camera and push the Record button to begin. You push the same button again when you're ready to stop filming. You connect your video camera to your computer and view the movie. You can even share it, easily, with people around the world.

What makes all this even better is that digital video cameras are easy to use and are very reasonably priced.

Now What?

There are many different digital video cameras on the market today, including such popular models as Cisco's Flip Video, Kodak's Play Touch camera, and Sony's Bloggie Touch camera. (The illustration shows three versions of the Flip Video.) You can find many models at

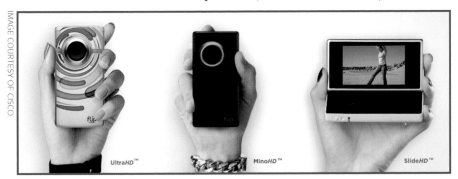

retail stores such as Best Buy and Walmart. Amazon, at http://www. amazon.com/, is also a good place to purchase digital video cameras.

Although, of course, each brand and camera model offers different features, most digital video cameras work in very similar ways. In this chapter, I'll show you how to use the very popular Flip Video camera.

What's So Great About Digital Video Cameras?

I love my Flip Video, and my teacher friends who use similar tools rave about them, too. Here are some of the reasons.

- Digital video cameras are convenient. Lightweight and small, they'll easily fit in your pocket or purse.
- They're uncomplicated. Typically, you just touch a single button to begin and end recording.
- They're easy to use. We teachers have enough to worry about without trying to figure out technology hassles. These cameras make it a snap to upload movies to sites such as YouTube™ and Facebook, or to e-mail them to friends.

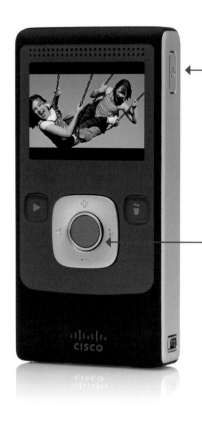

LIGHTS, CAMERA, ACTION!

1. Filming is a snap with the Flip. To turn it on, push the small rectangular button on the side of the camera. The screen will light up. Look at the screen to see what you're filming.

2. Under the screen is a big red button with a plus sign above it and a minus sign below it. To zoom in, push the plus sign. To zoom out, push the minus sign. To start recording, push the red button. To stop recording, push the red button again. That's it!

IT'S A WRAP

1. To review the videos you've filmed, use the arrow keys next to the red button to select the video you want to see. Then press the Play button.

2. To delete a video, use the arrow keys to select the video and then press the button with the icon of a Trashcan. A message will appear to ask if you want to delete this video or all the videos on the camera. Use the small arrow buttons to move to the answer you want: Yes, No, All. Then push the arrow button that sits to the left to say OK.

SHOWTIME!

1. Now you're ready to save the video to your computer so you can view it and share it. Look on the side of your Flip. Locate the button that has some dots on it. Slide this button down and the USB arm pops out.

IMAGE COURTESY OF CISCO.

2. Find a USB port on your computer and plug in the arm. Immediately you should see the Flip software appear. The tool-bar at the bottom of the screen will help you save your videos, share them, and even create a movie or snapshot.

3. Notice that an image from each of the videos you recorded is displayed on the screen above the toolbar. Click on the video or videos you want to save to your computer.

IMAGE COURTESY OF CISCO

4. Now click on the icon that looks like the Flip with a big arrow pointing to the computer. This will save your vid-eos to a Flip folder within your My Videos folder that's in your Documents folder on your computer.

IMAGE COURTESY OF CISCO

5. To put several videos together or to add a title and other features to your video, click on the Movie icon under Create. You'll be prompted to drag your video clips and place them in the order you want.

6. Click on Magic Movie if you want the software to put the clips together for you, or click on Full Length if you want to create your own movie. Simply follow the directions on each slide until you have published your movie.

Create Movie

Add and order items
Step 1 of 4: Add and reorder items for your movie.

Video 15   Video 14

1st   2nd

0:06   0:08

Add items by dragging them from the main window

Cancel   Magic Movie   Full Length

7. To share the movie, or just the video you filmed, look in the Share section of the toolbar. You can e-mail it, send it to a group, share it as a greeting card, or post it online to popular sites such as Facebook and YouTube™. Make sure you understand your school's policy for posting student work online.

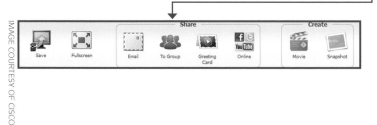

8. Many folks like to take their Flip Video footage and use it with other editing software such as Movie Maker, iMovie, or Pinnacle Studio. The only snag is sometimes the format of the Flip video may not work with your editing software. Double check what format your software needs.

9. Flip video is saved as an MP4. Movie Maker requires WMV format. You may have to convert or change the format of the video if necessary. There are many free online converters. One I like is Movavi, at http://online.movavi.com/.

So, you can use the Flip in the most basic way or spice it up with more advanced editing software. The choice is yours!

Let Me Show You

LESSON **1** Talk Show

Students work together to plan, research, write, and produce a talk show or newscast based on a controversial concept, such as gun control or global warming.

1. Before class, find video clips of talk shows and newscasts that will help your students understand the structure of news programs. To find clips, visit CNN Student News at http://www.cnn.com/studentnews/, or visit iTunes and download podcasts of news programs (see page 83 to learn how).

2. Show students the clips. Lead a class discussion about the structure of the news shows. Important features for them to notice include engaging lead-ins to stories, short and concise stories that answer the five Ws (who?, what?, when?, where?, and why?), and well-chosen words to describe the events.

3. Break the class into groups of three or four. Assign each group a topic. Explain to students that they will first research their topic and then write and film a news show featuring their topic.

4. A successful learning project requires scaffolding and planning. Break the task into bite-size pieces so students can accomplish them and understand the content and process.

5. Provide clear expectations, graphic organizers, planning sheets, checklists, and deadlines. You can help students stay on track if you require them to complete the planning piece first, before they begin the project.

6. Once students have completed their research, show them how to create a storyboard. Explain that the function of a storyboard is to help them organize their show or newscast scene-by-scene. Once students have completed the storyboard and you've approved it, they write the script.

Storyboard

Introduction:	Scene 1:	Scene 2:
Welcome to the show Introduce topic of global warming and guests	Discuss the basics of global warming	Experts talk about the effects of global warming
Scene 3:	**Scene 4:**	**Scene 5:**
Experts debate the issue of global warming	Experts answer questions from the audience	The host summarizes the issue and con-cludes the show

7. Students should rehearse their script until they're fluent. As they're working, make sure to guide them through the process. Help them pace themselves so that they'll be prepared for filming day.

8. Either have the students film each other, or you can film their productions.

9. Showtime! Let the whole class view each of the final productions. Ask students to complete an informal assessment of each production, deciding if each group presented the content well, appeared prepared, and moved through their script fluently. Share the feedback with each group.

LESSON **2** Self-Assessment

Include your students in the process of self-assessment by using the Flip Video to capture performances and provide reflection time after viewing. This is a great resource for teachers of the fine arts or physical education.

1. Imagine you're the drama teacher and you've been working with your students on performing monologues. You've modeled quality monologues. You've shown videos of actors performing monologues and you've given students the task of finding and performing a monologue.

2. Film the student performances of the monologues.

3. Have students watch their performances on the computer or the Flip Video itself and complete a written reflection. They may need to watch it multiple times to evaluate their physical movements, voice quality, and effectiveness.

4. Provide opportunity for students to rehearse some more and improve their performance based on what they viewed in the video.

5. This exercise works well even if you're not the drama teacher. Instead of filming a monologue, you could film students presenting a project or speech and then allow them the same self-assessment opportunity.

Get Real

I was told a long time ago, "The one doing most of the work is the one doing most of the learning." I find this to be very true. When students are allowed to take on roles and responsibilities, they actually learn more. Students are very creative and eager to accomplish real tasks. They probably understand media better than we do. So let them take the reins. Digital video cameras are so easy to use and the software is so simple, students of just about any age can film and create movies. I've used the Flip with kindergarten kids as well as high school students. You know what I've found? Every time I challenge students to put their talents to work, they rise to my expectations. In fact, they usually far exceed what I had envisioned.

If it's possible, borrow other video recorders so several groups can record on the same day at the same time in different locations of the room or in the hall outside the room, if that's allowed. If you have parents who like to volunteer or older students who buddy up with your class, use those experienced helpers to assist students in rehearsing, filming, or editing.

So early on, young people get the kinds of feedback that used to be available only to professionals, and only rarely to students. This is enormously appealing to today's young people . . . . Students who get hundreds or thousands of hits on their video, or hundreds of comments (or none) on a web post, truly know where they stand—not just in school, but in the real world.

—MARC PRENSKY (2010)

Everyone wants to be a star. That's not exactly true. I've seen students who don't like the attention focused on them blossom when they're the directors or videographers for particular projects. It's not necessary to have every student in front of the camera. It's okay to allow students to work behind the scenes to complete the task. It'll be a more enjoyable experience for everyone.

In a classroom with one computer, a schedule will need to be implemented to provide each individual or group of students with time to load their video footage and edit it. Do set time-limit requirements for multimedia projects. A video of no more than five minutes is best. In my experience, after a couple of minutes the audience tends to lose interest. Working within the guidelines of three to five minutes gives plenty of time to convey learning and content.

Podcasts & Yodio

I vividly remember my first iPod purchase. It was my son's birthday and I wanted to get him something really special. The iPod had just shown up on the scene and was still pretty pricey, but I knew he'd love it since he was crazy about listening to music. I bought it hoping that my digital native would know how to use it. That he did! He quickly learned how to download music and podcasts. Needless to say, since that time, I have purchased quite a few more iPods due to improvements in the technology and the need for everyone in our household to have one.

So why have the iPod and other MP3 players become the devices we think of when we want to jam to our favorite tunes? I think it's the size and portability of the iPod that make it so attractive. In my day we had the Walkman, and we thought we were so cool with those headphones and that cassette player clipped to our acid-washed jeans. But, you were sunk if the cassette tape got jammed and you sure couldn't hide that big box sitting on your hip. The iPod has not only decreased the size of the player, it's eliminated the need for cassettes and CDs. It can hold literally hundreds of audio recordings instead of just a select few songs, and it even has a video screen.

Because of the iPod's popularity and its ability to store so much information, people started thinking about new ways to use the device. Hence, the podcast. News organizations, media critics, college professors, and anyone with a passion for their hobby or group can now record their messages, and others can download them from the Internet and listen to them on their iPods.

A podcast is a recording similar to a radio show. In fact, many popular radio shows are available as podcasts. There are three kinds of podcasts: audio, enhanced, and vodcast or video. An audio podcast is an audio recording of talking, music, and sounds. An enhanced podcast mixes some images with the audio, and the vodcast or video is a multimedia presentation with moving images and audio.

Now What?

Have you ever listened to a podcast? Even if you don't have an iPod or MP3 player, you can still try it. You can listen on your computer. Probably the most popular place to find podcasts is on iTunes. The great thing about finding podcasts on iTunes is that they're usually free. Video may have a cost, but most basic podcasts are available at no cost.

COURTESY OF APPLE

ACCESSING PODCASTS

The first thing you'll want to do is to make sure iTunes is loaded on your classroom computer because that's where you'll go to purchase podcasts. When you load iTunes, you'll also set up a password and username that allow you to purchase items. To download iTunes, go to http://www. apple.com/itunes/. You may need a technician to help you with this because you probably don't have permission to download a program onto your computer.

1. Once iTunes is downloaded, it'll be listed in your programs or as an icon on the desktop. When you need it, you'll just double click on that icon.

2. Look to the left of your iTunes screen and find the icon that looks like a shopping bag. Click on it to go to the iTunes Store.

3. Look across the screen until you find Podcasts. Click on Podcasts. Here you can search for any topic you'd like. You can search by looking for Audio Podcasts or Video. Type the subject you want in the search bar.

4. Once you find a podcast you like, you can listen to it or watch it by clicking on the title. Just for fun, check out a few episodes to see what it's like. Are you amazed at all the things available through podcasts?

5. What types of podcasts might be helpful to your students? There are podcasts that discuss science topics, critique literature, teach foreign languages, and even offer sports tutorials.

6. When you find a podcast that you want to download to your iPod, click on Buy or Subscribe, even if it's free. The podcast then will be loaded to your iTunes account.

7. If you subscribe to a podcast, that means all future podcasts in the series will automatically be downloaded to your iTunes account. Of course you can unsubscribe any time you want to.

8. A pop-up window will appear asking for your password and for you to verify the purchase. So, if you happen to click on something that you don't want, don't worry. You have to okay the purchase before you're charged.

MAKING PODCASTS AVAILABLE TO STUDENTS

At this point you might be thinking, "Okay? So what do I do once I have the podcasts?" The goal is to use podcasts as a tool to reteach a concept, provide extra practice, or enrich the content. You'll want to make the podcasts available to students so they can listen to or watch them either at home, on the class computer, or through iPods.

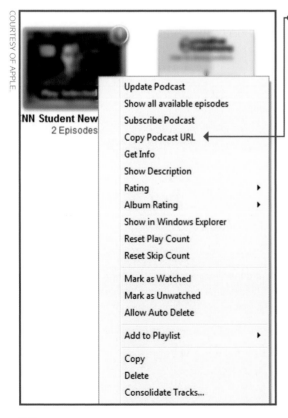

COURTESY OF APPLE.

1. If you want students to access the podcasts at home, right click the icon of the podcast you want. (If you have a one button mouse, hold down the control key and click.) It has an option that says Copy Podcast URL. Click on it to paste the URL or address to your blog or website.

2. If you're still sending paper copies of newsletters, copy and paste the URL or web address to your newsletter so students can locate it at home.

3. If you want to make the podcast available in class, show students how to click on the iTunes icon on the computer and locate the podcast. If you're not allowed to load iTunes onto your computer, then link the podcast URL to your website or blog and access it from there.

4. If you have iPods in the classroom for students to use, download the podcasts to them. To do this, click on each podcast you want to load onto the iPods.

5. Plug an iPod into your computer using the cord provided. Immediately a message will appear on your screen to tell you that the iPod is syncing with your iTunes and not to unplug.

6. All of the items you selected from your iTunes account are being loaded onto the iPod.

7. You'll need to do this with each iPod. When the process is complete, a window will appear with a message to tell you the download is complete and you can now safely disconnect the iPod from your computer.

AH, THE OPPORTUNITIES!

So far I've only shown you how to download existing podcasts. Well, guess what? Now you're going to learn how to create your own podcasts. Just think of the possibilities! You can record important lessons that you know always give students trouble, and they can review the information again and again until it's clear. You can create podcasts featuring your back-to-school information so parents can listen at their convenience. More importantly, think about how students can create their own podcasts to express what they know and have learned. Each month as your class reads various novels, students can create podcasts to discuss the theme, author's purpose, and quality of the writing. This might just motivate other students to read those books. It'll also keep the students creating the podcast on track with their own reading.

Sounds like this has possibilities, doesn't it? It could replace some of the paper and pencil things you've been doing. Ready to learn more? Well, there's the "I have no equipment" way or the "I have access to a microphone, and I can download some software" way. Which is the right one for you?

MAKING THEM YOURSELF—THE LOW/NO-TECH WAY

Let's go with the "I have no equipment" way first. Meet Yodio. This free tool uses a phone to record your podcasts and will even store them online if you don't have any place to put them. Now you don't have to worry about getting a microphone or downloading any software. You just register and get started.

1. Go to Yodio at http://www.yodio.com/ and click on the Join button. Complete the registration page. Make sure to include the phone number of the primary phone you and your students will be using to make the podcast. It can be a cell phone or a landline.

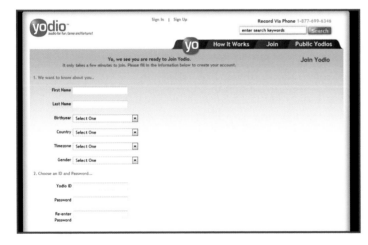

2. Your registration will be sent to the e-mail account you used to register. You must open that e-mail first and click on the provided link to activate the account.

3. When you're ready to record, log on to your Yodio account. Call 1-877-MY-YODIO (1-877-699-6346) to record your podcast. Follow all the prompts to record.

4. Once you're finished recording, go back to your Yodio account on your

computer and put your podcast together.

5. You can insert an image if you'd like. Click on the tab that says Image. Find the box that says Upload Images. Click on that box. Browse your files, select the picture you want, and then click the Open button. Your image is uploaded.

6. Look at the tabs again. Click on Create Yodio. Now you'll see a screen with the option to create a standard blank Yodio. Click on that box and you'll be moved to another screen with all the tools you'll need to make your Yodio.

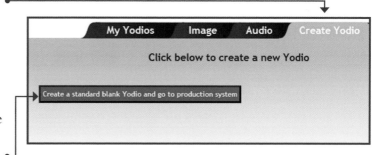

7. You should see some new tabs at the top of the screen. One says Choose Images; the other says Choose Audio. You'll find your recording in the Choose Audio tab. If you want to add music, you can go to that tab and upload music to use.

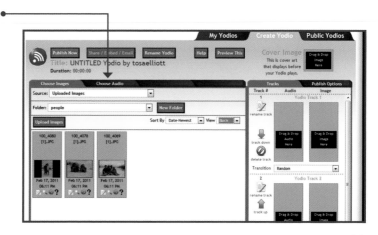

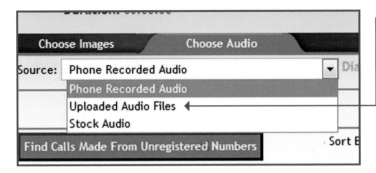

8. To add music, click on the arrow next to Phone Recorded Audio and choose Uploaded Audio Files. Browse your documents to find the folder with your MP3 audio files. Click on the file you want and then click on Open.

9. Take a look to the right of your screen. You're ready to put things together. Simply drag and drop the audio recording you want to use onto the blue box that says Drag and Drop Audio Here.

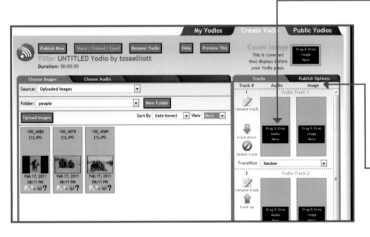

10. Now click on the Images tab. Drag and drop the image you would like to use onto the blue box that says Drag and Drop Image Here.

11. Remember that music you just saved? Click on the Add Another Track button under the drag and drop boxes. You'll see new boxes appear. Just drag your music selection onto the new box that says Drag and Drop Audio.

12. You're almost there! Click on the Publish

Options button. Here you'll need to name your Yodio and fill in basic information about the recording. When you have it completed, click on the Publish Now button.

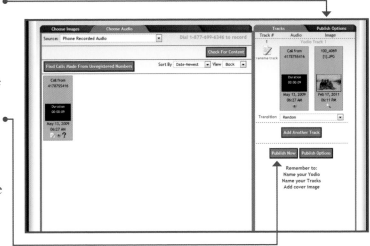

13. Awesome! You're now a podcaster! Way to go. Now you can share the amazing podcast you or your students made. Click on Share to see all of your options.

14. You can e-mail the link to someone. You can copy the embedding code listed on the left-hand side of the Share Box and paste it on the html section of your website or blog (see page 134 for how to embed html code to a blog).

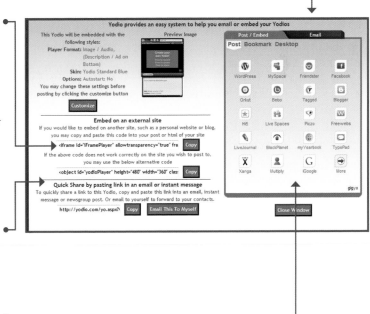

15. You can also choose to copy the link and publish it in your newsletter. Just look for Quick Share and click on Copy to get the URL for your now published Yodio.

16. You can click on the icons to the right of the screen and your podcast will automatically be linked to your Facebook or Twitter page.

MAKING THEM YOURSELF—THE MORE-TECH WAY

Option number 2 for creating a podcast will take a little software and a little equipment.

You'll need a microphone. I prefer the headset type for my students so they can hear themselves while talking; plus it eliminates noises from around the room. You can purchase headsets with mics anywhere electronics are sold. They range in cost from $15 to hundreds of dollars. For my budget, I've purchased the lower cost sets and have been satisfied with their performance for how we use them.

If you're a PC user you'll need to download Audacity software to record. You'll also need LAME, which is another program listed on Audacity. It adds a feature so your recording will be in MP3 format. You must select it in addition to Audacity. Both programs are free to download and don't take much time. Go to Audacity at http://audacity.sourceforge.net/. Again, if you're downloading to your computer at school, it's likely that you'll need a technician to help you.

If you're a Mac user, you should already have Garage Band on your computer that will allow you to record. If not, go to http://www.apple.com/ilife/garageband/ for help.

Both Garage Band and Audacity work in similar ways:

1. Open your recording software, either Garage Band or Audacity.

2. Plug in your microphone or make sure your built-in one is working correctly.

3. Locate the Record and Stop buttons in your software.

4. Click on the Record button and begin talking. Click on the Stop button when you're finished.

5. If you want to add music you have saved on your computer, click on Import Audio. Browse your computer for the music you want to use and then click on Open.

6. Next you'll trim and cut your recording and music to your liking. You can also adjust the volume of each so they're balanced. Each program works differently, so follow the instructions provided with your software.

7. Once you're finished editing, save the recording. To do this, go to the File option on the menu bar at the top of the screen. Click on

File and then click on Save As. Choose Export as MP3 to finish the process.

SHARING YOUR PODCASTS

Now it's time to decide where to put these podcasts. Mac users can upload to iTunes through Garage Band. That's pretty nifty. PC users can also upload to iTunes or place work on another podcasting site, such as Podomatic at http://www.podomatic.com/ or PodBean at http://www.podbean.com/. Putting your podcasts on any of these sites allows you a quick way to share them—either to your own blog, website, class computer, or iPods.

Always be cautious when posting student work to the Internet. Make sure you understand your school's policy for technology. Some districts don't allow student images or work to be posted online. Other schools allow it if parents have been made aware and have signed a document giving permission. The sites mentioned above do allow you to make the podcasts private.

Decision time. Which way of creating podcasts will work for you and your students? The answer should be the one that's easiest and most time efficient for your schedule.

Let Me Show You

Now that we're past the technical side of things, let's focus on what's most important. How are we going use this technology tool with students? The first tip I want to share is this: *don't wing it*. Just as videos aren't very productive if we don't prepare first, podcasts are boring and lifeless without proper prep time.

BASICS FOR ANY LESSON

To create podcasts with your students remember these four steps:

1. Plan
2. Record
3. Produce
4. Publish

LET'S GO INTO THESE STEPS IN A LITTLE MORE DETAIL

1. You must require students to complete a plan before they record. Look at the sample graphic organizer provided here.

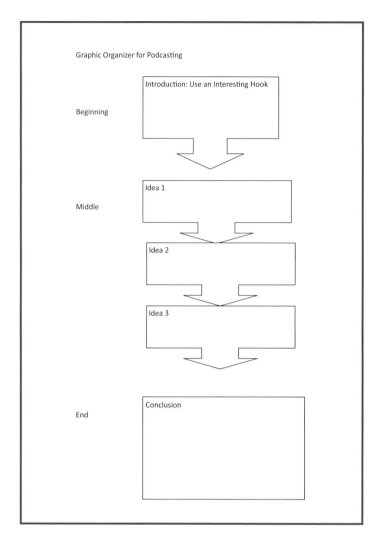

Graphic Organizer for Podcasting

Beginning

Introduction: Use an Interesting Hook

Middle

Idea 1

Idea 2

Idea 3

End

Conclusion

2. Notice how the organizer guides students from the introduction to the conclusion. The focus is on content.

3. After you have approved the plan, give students time to rehearse. They will be more fluent and that will make it easier for the audience to pay attention.

4. Recording may take more than one try to get correct. Make sure everything is set up and ready to go prior to students arriving in class on recording day.

5. Produce means to put it together. If you used Yodio, have students help put the image and tracks together. If you used recording software, let students edit and add music.

6. Publishing allows students to take all their hard work and share it with the world. As quickly as possible, publish the podcast to iTunes or another site. If there is too much lag time after producing, we tend to forget and the students feel their efforts are not important.

LESSON How To . . .

Help your students understand the importance of using specific details in their writing and speaking by creating "How To" podcasts.

1. Demonstrate how to do a certain procedure, for example how to make no-bake cookies or how to paint your fingernails.

2. Ask students to list what steps would be necessary in order to replicate the procedure you just demonstrated.

3. Discuss the importance of using details and the correct sequence when writing or speaking.

4. Challenge students to teach the class how to do something. Have each student select something he feels he's expert at and could successfully talk others through the process of doing. It could be as simple as how to wrap a gift or more complicated, such as how to repair a bicycle.

5. Share with students the requirements and rubric for completing the podcast. Emphasize that just describing how to do something isn't enough.

6. Their directions must also have an element of creativity so that the audience isn't just listening to steps. The goal is not only to give information, but to get the audience interested in the topic.

7. Students must write out the directions for completing their tasks. They also need to plan transitions or novelty ideas to make the podcast more interesting for the audience.

8. Students can rehearse with a partner to see if the other person can complete the task or if they need to revise their steps.

9. Record, produce, and publish the How To podcasts.

10. Give students the opportunity to listen to several of the podcasts and try to follow the directions for one of the How To podcasts. Students trying to replicate the How To should provide feedback to the author.

11. Each student will take the feedback given by others and revise their writing and podcast.

12. If time allows, have students record, produce, and publish the second, revised podcasts also.

Get Real

iTunes isn't the only place to find podcasts. You may also want to check out The EPN Web at http://www.epnweb.org/ and Educational Feeds at http://www.educational-feeds.com/.

Creating podcasts is a brand new skill for most teachers. Start with what seems most comfortable. This probably means using Yodio at first. Most of us know how to use our cell phones, and we don't have to spend money to create this type of podcast.

> For teaching to be effective, students need to talk about what they are learning. This is because when talking about a topic, they must first think about and mentally process the information. As they discuss the content, they verbally process the ideas. As a result, they come to a better, deeper, and more complete understanding of what they are studying.
>
> —RICHARD ALLEN (2010)

Set deadlines for completing podcasts. It's going to take time to plan, record, produce, and publish, so make sure the content is valuable enough to justify spending the amount of time necessary to work on the project. In other words, don't do podcasts just to do podcasts. Podcasts should review, enhance, or reteach the content.

Instead of a weekly class newsletter, consider creating a podcast. Middle and high school teachers can save lots of time by producing a podcast for each semester that outlines the goals and expectations of the course. With so many sections of students, a podcast could really help you avoid having to repeat things over and over.

Podcast yourself teaching. You spent a lot of time putting together your lecture or direct instruction. Why not podcast that teaching for your students and parents to use at home while studying?

Skype

My favorite cartoons of all time have to be the Flintstones and the Jetsons. Quite a difference between the two, but I love the characters and the wacky doodads they use to get things accomplished. When I started to use Skype, I really thought I was living in the time of the Jetsons. How weird is it to talk to people in another state or country and be able to see and hear them in real time? Amazing! Skype is a free program you can download to your computer to call and talk to anyone in the world. You can use a webcam with Skype to see and hear the other person or just use a microphone to talk to them.

Our son is in college, and, just as many college kids do, he applied for an internship in another state. Now, even though it was a while back, I remember when I was applying for jobs. There was the process of delivering the résumé in person, waiting for a phone call to schedule an interview, getting dressed up and driving to the interview, and then waiting for that letter or phone call with the decision. Not true anymore. The process was very different for Austin.

He first submitted his electronic résumé online. Then, he was contacted on his cell phone and asked to "friend" this organization on Facebook (so they could check him out, I guess). He was then interviewed from his home by a panel using Skype. That's right.

With the simple connection of a webcam, the panel and Austin were able to see and interact with each other. Within a few hours he received a text saying he had the internship. Calling all Jetsons!

I was just amazed and impressed by the whole process of getting a job in today's digital world. My son was not. He looked at the Facebook friendship, the Skyping, and the texting as just what you do to get things accomplished. Once again, because of living with my own digital native, I was reminded how useful technology can be in the classroom. Using Skype can help my students connect with other students around the world, experts in science, even favorite authors.

Now What?

You'll need to join Skype, create a name so others will be able to contact you, and then download the Skype software. It's free, and downloading will take just a few minutes. If you're downloading to your computer at school, you may need a technician to help you with this because it's unlikely you have permission to download a program onto your computer.

GET READY TO SKYPE

1. Go to Skype at http://www.skype.com/. At the top of the screen you'll see a Join Skype button. Click on it to get to the registration page. Fill in the information and then click on the I Agree and Continue button at the bottom of the page.

2. Now you're ready to download Skype to your computer. Choose the type of Skype you need based on your brand of computer, and then click on Download Skype.

Create an account or sign in

It only takes a minute or two - then you'll be ready to call your friends for free once you've downloaded and installed Skype.

Sign in   Create an account

First name*   Last name*

Your email address*   Repeat email*

Note: no-one can see your email address.

3. Once Skype is downloaded, it'll be listed in your programs or as an icon on the desktop. When you need it, just double click on that icon.

4. To call someone on Skype, you first must make the person a contact. Look at your menu bar and find Contacts. When you click on this you'll see a drop-down menu. Select Add a Contact. You'll need to know either the person's e-mail or Skype name to add them as a contact.

5. Before calling someone on Skype with your class, you'll probably want to arrange a time that's mutually convenient to have the session.

6. When you're ready to call, click on the contact you want to chat with. Now select the Green Call button to connect you and the contact. Turn on the webcam by clicking the My Video icon. If you only want to type and chat, look for the icon that has a talk bubble. To hang up, click on End Call.

WHO YOU GONNA CALL?

How can you use Skype to connect with other classrooms and experts?

1. Skype has created a site just for teachers called Skype in the Classroom. Find it at http://education. skype.com/. You can register for free and become part of a database of educators who want to find people to Skype with.

2. For example, if you teach 6th grade science, you can register and find other 6th grade classrooms across the U.S. and the world with whom your students can share ideas and experiments. Prior to the creation of this site, it was quite a challenge to find other classrooms willing to Skype.

3. Another site that's wonderful is Skype an Author Network at http://skypeanauthor.wetpaint.com/. Their mission is to provide K–12 teachers with a way to connect authors and readers through virtual visits.

4. Most authors participating in Skype sessions allow a very limited amount of time per session, so it's important to be organized and know what questions your students want to ask.

5. I've also noticed when I visit the web pages of my students' favorite authors I'm usually able to find out if they're available to Skype. Many authors are now found on sites such as Twitter, Facebook, YouTube™, and Flickr.

6. It's worth the effort to check out authors' web pages and join their social networking opportunities. You get personal insight into their work and learn about their upcoming projects. Try it out!

7. To find contacts you might also look closer to home. Ask a colleague in another classroom to Skype with you and your students. E-mail local officials or college professors with some type of expertise that would benefit your students and arrange to Skype with them.

STEPS TO A SUCCESSFUL SKYPE SESSION

1. Have a clear purpose and objective for the Skype session. If you want to learn about culture, Skype with a class in another country. If you want to help students understand rocks and minerals, Skype with the geologist at the local university.

2. Make sure to have the webcam or microphone set up prior to students arriving in class. Have the contacts already entered, so all you have to do is call.

3. Prepare a note-taking sheet and have any manipulatives available to students that they might need during the Skype session.

4. Practice the process of Skyping often.

5. Hold students accountable for the discussion and information presented during the Skype session. Will they use the session for research? Will they create a product after the session? Will there be a quiz or just a class discussion?

6. Students should understand the purpose of the Skype session and be responsible for the content following the experience.

Let Me Show You

LESSON Buddy Up

Older students will learn how to organize and effectively present information as they instruct younger students via Skype. You may have high school students teach elementary students or middle school students teach kindergarten students. Both groups are sure to enjoy the process.

1. Ahead of time, work with your buddy teacher to determine a set of content objectives that align to both age groups For example, the high school students may be working with high levels of algebra or geometry, but the elementary students need to know the basics of those subject areas.

2. Have the older students prepare lessons to share via Skype. You may want to have the whole class involved with the Skype session, or if you have enough computers and webcams, you might place students in small groups to teach learners who will also be placed in small groups.

3. To make the session more interactive, the older students should lead the younger ones through a series of tasks. Perhaps they can play trivia games, or the younger students can complete a graph or diagram with the older students leading them through the process.

4. Older students must prepare a plan and rehearse with peers. Emphasize how important it is for them to have questions to ask, stories to tell, and step-by-step directions for activities, such as filling in a map.

5. Prior to Skype day, practice using the equipment. Make sure the webcam is functioning, and the sound quality is good. Do trial runs with the other class to make sure the Skype connection is working.

6. On Skype Day, the younger students will learn from the older students.

7. Both groups will complete an assessment after the Skype experience. The younger students can display what they've learned through their graphs or diagrams.

8. The older students should be held accountable for the content by taking a test. Mastery of the communication component is recognized by their receiving a score based on a rubric.

Get Real

Skype is a wonderful tool for the classroom. We can bring the world to our students without leaving our seats. However, just as with cell phones, Skype calls can get dropped. Due to the amount of Internet activity in your school or with the contact's connection, you might lose the call. Don't worry, just call back. If you know your school often has a slow Internet connection when everyone's using it, you might ask your colleagues to avoid using the Internet for the 15 to 20 minutes that you'll be using Skype. Skyping also requires streaming. This means that the video is playing online. This can take up lots of bandwidth, or space, which can make things run slowly or get dropped all together. Make sure to try things out early and be ready to try again if this happens.

> We can no longer ask our children to live in a world where they are immersed in technology in all parts of their lives except when they go to school.
>
> —LARRY ROSEN (2010)

Webcams are so handy, and the experience of Skyping is really enhanced when we can see each other as we talk. Choose a good quality webcam that's easy to operate. My favorite right now is the HUE webcam by Clique. It has a moveable neck so you can turn it to see the entire class or keep it focused on just one area of the classroom. The HUE is very affordable, ranging from $30 to over $100. You can find HUE webcams on Amazon at http://www.amazon.com/.

Get Busy:
Web Tools That Make Everyone's Life Easier

I remember when I was in high school and wanted to know what time *The Breakfast Club* was playing at the local movie theater. I'd search the house for the newspaper, and, if it couldn't be found, then I'd call the theater and wait for what seemed like hours to listen to all the showings and times. Good grief! It took forever and it really stunk if for some reason you hit the wrong button on the recording menu—you'd have to start all over again. Next I'd make calls to all of my friends, hoping not to hear the dreaded busy signal to inform them of the Friday night plans. Nowadays, you don't really need to go to the movie theater at all. You can use the Internet to view the latest flicks. And if you do want a night out, you can grab your iPhone or laptop and, within a second or two, you can know exactly what movies are playing, when, and where. Just text your BFFs and you're good to go. Things have certainly changed.

Now think about schools. What's the one thing every teacher seems to want? What do we grumble and complain about as we sit through yet another faculty meeting or workshop? Time. We want more of it, and there's never enough of it to accomplish all that we're asked to do. Do you ever wonder if students feel the same way? Think about the routines of your students. Their days are filled with hours in school, homework, sports or music practice, family and church responsibilities, and the list goes on. I guess we're all in this together, students and teachers. We both need time to accomplish what we must do, and we both want time to have a life.

Is technology the answer to this problem? It could be. When you find effective tools that help you work or learn better and more quickly, then you may want to consider using them. The Internet has changed tremendously since its initial appearance in our homes. Years ago the World Wide Web was used to find information or to let us see places we'd never been. It was amazing stuff back then. It truly opened the world to us. Now, WWW means something very different: it represents Whatever, Whenever, Wherever. Instead of only observing or visiting, we can actually create and interact with people and material on the web.

This whole idea of whatever, whenever, wherever really started to make sense to me a few years back. I'd just started teaching online courses. As an online instructor I had to agree to be available to answer questions and provide feedback to my students quickly. I was having no trouble with this commitment until I wanted to go on vacation with my family. We were going on a cruise and would be gone a week, so I had to find a way to keep up with the course. Luckily the cruise ship was equipped with an Internet café that I could visit throughout my trip. I was able to maintain my conversations with my students even though I was thousands of miles away sitting in the middle of the ocean. Talk about whatever, whenever, wherever. My students from all over the U.S. and the world could learn at their convenience about the topic I was teaching, and I could teach it while sailing to another country. Incredible!

The iGeneration of Learners and Teachers

What's so interesting about students today is they really desire to do things on their own time schedules. They know they can access just about anything they need no matter what time of day it is. Whether they're on their laptops or using their smart phones or iPads, they have access to more information and can get that information in much less time than any generation has been able to do before them. I've found that teachers are becoming more and more like our students in this area. Time is valuable, so perhaps you prefer to get your professional development or faculty updates through technology in some way. Instead of lugging around a lesson plan book, calendar, and day planner, you may be using apps and free web tools to organize your schedules, responsibilities, and goals.

Social networking has changed the way people communicate. Sites like Facebook and Twitter help friends and colleagues stay current. Very young students interact online with each other on kid-friendly sites such as Club Penguin and WebKinz. Educators are following each other on Twitter to share ideas and resources and even debate educational philosophy. Teens, parents, and even grandparents are posting on each other's Facebook walls and accepting friendships from people they've known for years and some they may have just met.

We're a very social society these days, and the prediction is that social networking will continue to grow and be the way we share information about everything from our favorite restaurants and celebrities to how to balance the budget.

So, are you ready to bring these tools into your classroom? This section provides you with time-saving resources to help you connect with others and get organized. You'll learn how to post homework assignments and discussion questions online. You'll learn how to create online binders chock-full of information and resources that students, parents, or colleagues can access 24/7. You'll even learn how to publish your very own blog!

Plus, you'll learn about some pretty nifty tools to help your students organize their thinking and learning in really creative ways. Students will love using digital sticky notes, creating online multimedia posters, and presenting their research in dynamic new ways using tools such as Prezi. But as I've said again and again, it's really not about the technology. As cool as all of these tools are, they're meaningful only if they're used to teach your students how to clearly communicate and effectively share their thoughts, ideas, and opinions. With your scaffolding of instruction and your clear purpose in mind, students will learn and achieve.

authorSTREAM and PowerPoint

Imagine that your students have worked for weeks on a research project about Going Green. They've created a truly amazing PowerPoint presentation. You're so proud of their findings and solutions for making your community a better place to live. What a letdown that their PowerPoint presentation will be viewed only once by a small audience. What if you could place their PowerPoint presentation online and invite your community leaders, mayor, and city council members to view it and provide feedback? Real learning would certainly be taking place.

And what if there were a way that students could somehow view the PowerPoint presentation they missed while absent? Or if there were a way students could go back again and again to view the PowerPoint presentation you created outlining the causes of World War II so they could review the ideas and dates? Don't you think that would be pretty neat? Let's be honest: no matter how amazing your PowerPoint presentation is, students won't retain all of the ideas and information you present to them in one lesson.

Well, guess what? You can easily make PowerPoint presentations available 24/7 online so a wider audience can appreciate and learn from them (and even interact with them by leaving feedback) with a simple to use and free tool called authorSTREAM.

Now What?

1. Go to author-
STREAM at http://www.
authorstream.com/. Scan
the top of the screen.
You'll see an orange but-
ton that says Join Now.
Click that button, and
the registration page will
appear. Fill in your information, and then click on
the Join Now button.

2. Read across the top
of the new screen that
appears until you find the
orange Upload button.
Run your mouse over the
button to activate a drop-
down menu.

3. This is where you'll
select how you want to
upload your presentations.
Most likely you'll use presentations already saved to
your computer, rather than
ones found on a website.

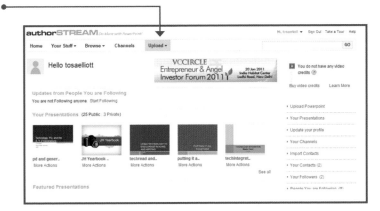

4. If you want to upload
multiple files at once,
choose Upload from
Desktop. If you have only
one file you want to use,
choose Single File Upload.
Let's walk through the
process of how to upload

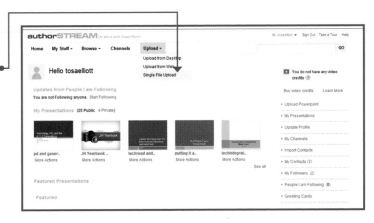

a single file from your computer.

5. Click on Single File Upload. The first step is to select your PowerPoint presentation (PPT). To do that, click on the Browse button. A small pop-up screen will appear. Use the drop-down menu at the top of this screen to locate your PPT.

6. For instance, if you saved the PPT in your My Documents folder, double click on the folder to display all of the items you've saved there. Scroll through the list until you find the presentation. Click on the PPT to select it, and then click on the Open button.

7. Once you've selected your PPT file, you'll be prompted to type in the title of the presentation, a description of it, and word tags that might help others find it. For example, if the PPT is about solving word problems, your tags might be *math*, *word problems*, and *problem-solving*.

8. Look at the Privacy Settings options. If you make the file Private, only

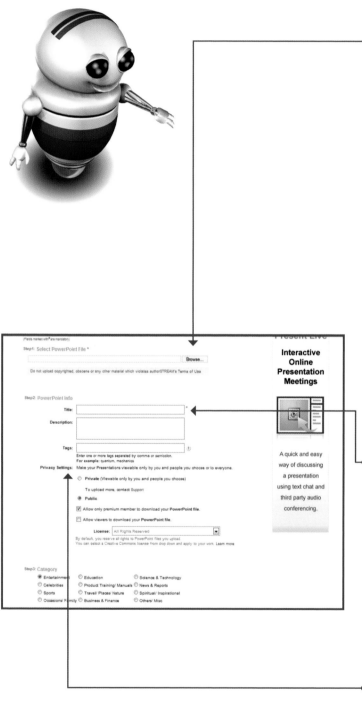

the individuals you select may view the PPT. That's generally a good choice when posting student work.

9. However, there may be times when you want to make the file Public so a wider audience can access the presentation. Consult your school's policy regarding posting student work online.

10. You'll need to decide if you want others to be able to download and save the PPT. Keep in mind copyright issues. For privacy and keeping ownership of your own or your students' work, you may want to eliminate the downloading option.

11. The final step is to select the category the presentation falls into. For most of us, that's Education. Now click on the gray Upload PowerPoint button. You're done!

12. Once the presentation appears in your account, it's ready to share with others. E-mail people the URL, copy the embed code and paste it into the html section of your website or blog (see page 134 to learn how), or click on the icons of Facebook or Twitter to post it to those sites.

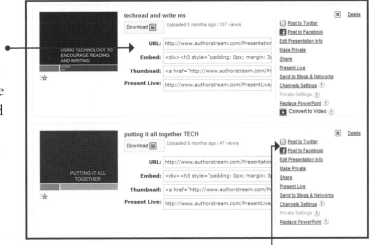

A Quick Refresher on the Basics of PowerPoint

Maybe you haven't created a PowerPoint presentation since college or the last school board meeting. Perhaps you have never asked students to create a PowerPoint presentation. I want to challenge you to use PowerPoint for your own instruction as well as making it available as a tool for students to use. It'll appeal to your visual learners and the process of creating one will help all students to organize their thinking.

PowerPoint is a Microsoft software product. It's not free and it's not web based. You purchase the software and download it to the computer. Most often people purchase a Microsoft Office bundle of software, which generally includes Word, Excel, and PowerPoint. Usually when schools purchase computers, they also purchase Power-Point and have it ready for students and teachers to use.

Once you have PowerPoint on your computer, you'll want to start using it. I have a few things I'd like to share with you that will make your presentations more effective. I've found when creating PowerPoint presentations and working with students that less is more. Fewer words, more visuals. Fewer bullets, more real pictures. Fewer wacky animations, more purposeful movement to keep folks focused on the content. Fewer distracting colors and fonts, more simple and clean-looking slides. The most successful PowerPoint presentations have a consistent look and are directly focused on the content, not the bells and whistles of the program.

The basics of PowerPoint creation are very simple, no matter what version you have. I'll be using PowerPoint 2007 for the explanation that follows. Whether you have a Mac or a PC, the 2007 version of PowerPoint will work in the same way.

LET'S GET STARTED

1. To begin a Power-Point presentation, locate the program. Either find it on your desktop or go to your Start menu and search in the Microsoft Office Folder in Programs for PowerPoint.

2. Click on the PowerPoint icon. The program will open to your title slide. The toolbar across the top is organized with tabs or called "ribbons." This is really handy because it allows you to access whatever you need quickly.

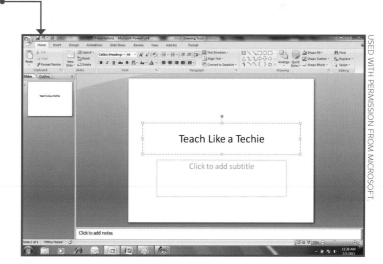

3. When you're working, PowerPoint actually opens the ribbon you'll probably need at that moment. For instance, if you're inserting a picture, the ribbon that helps you edit pictures is displayed. Of course if you need a tool on a different ribbon, you can just click to that ribbon.

ADD TEXT

1. Type in your title on the first slide. When you type on a slide, the rest of the Home ribbon provides you with options for selecting font, size, color, etc.

2. To add more slides, look on the Home ribbon and click on the New Slide icon. You can change the layout of each slide by selecting the slide you want to work with and then pulling down the arrow beside Layout in the Home ribbon.

3. You may want to use the same layout throughout the presentation. It depends on your content. I often choose the blank layout because I like to use lots of images and I want one good-sized image on each slide. Just click on the option that best meets your needs.

ADD IMAGES

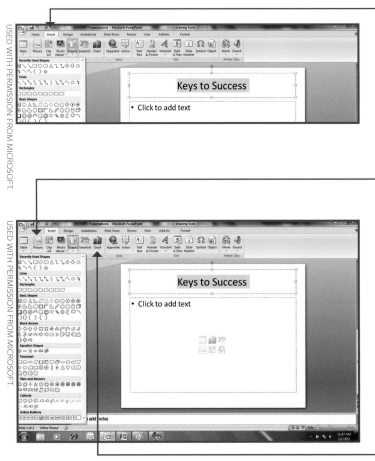

1. Now that you know how to add slides and work with text, click on the Insert ribbon. Here you'll find options for inserting shapes, pictures, charts, even video and sound.

2. When you want to insert a photo, click on the Picture icon. A pop-up window will open. You'll need to browse your computer for the image, click on it, and then click on Insert. The photo you selected will appear on your slide.

3. Inserting video and sound works in just the same manner.

4. To insert a chart, click on the chart icon. A whole menu of chart options will open. Click on the one you want to use and then click OK. Microsoft Excel will automatically open. Enter your data and resize the chart for the number of columns and rows you want. Excel will then automatically transform that data into a chart.

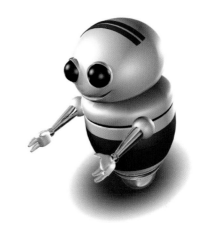

PUTTING IT ALL TOGETHER

1. Once you've created all of your slides, click on the Design ribbon. Here you'll see lots of options for the background of your presentation. Click on the one you'd like to use. You can keep changing the design until you find the one you like best.

2. To the right of the design options are Colors, Fonts, and Effects tools. Each one has a drop-down arrow with options. If you like a design, but want to change the color scheme, effect, or font, use the drop-down arrows to customize the design option you selected.

3. You can animate your presentation by clicking on the Animations ribbon. This allows you to give your text or an image some special effects. For example, if you want a title like, Archaeology Rocks! to come flying onto your slide, highlight the text and then click on the arrow next to No Animation and turn on the Fly In effect.

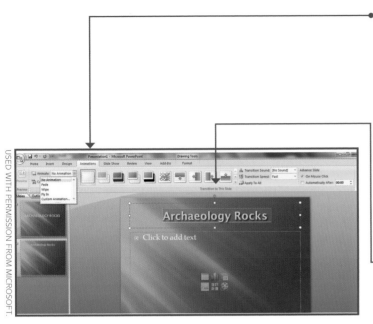

4. To transition from slide to slide in a certain way, select one of the transition options found in the middle of the Animations ribbon. For example, if you want to have a slide fade in, click on the image showing the Fade In option. To have all of the slides fade in, click on Apply To All.

5. Use the Slide Show ribbon to set up your show and begin your presentation. Click on Set Up Slide Show if you want to display each slide for a predetermined amount of time or if you want the slide show to run automatically without anyone clicking to advance to the next slide.

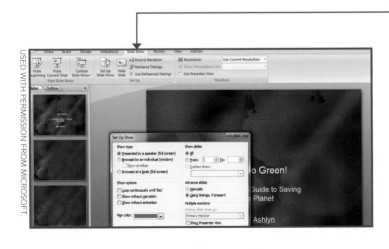

6. To view the presentation, click on From Beginning found on the top left of the Slide Show ribbon. Or, if you're working and you just want to see the presentation from where you are, click on From Current Slide.

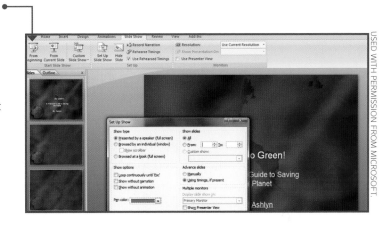

7. To save your PPT, go to the menu bar and click on File. Select Save As, name your PPT, and choose where you want to save the file. It's always a good idea to save your work frequently when working on any document.

Let Me Show You

LESSON Learning Is a Game

PowerPoint is perfect for creating interactive games. Students always enjoy a game of *Jeopardy* to review information, so let them create their own games for their classmates to play. It's a great way to have them prepare for an assessment.

1. Before class, visit PowerPoint Games at http://jc-schools.net/ tutorials/ppt-games/. This site provides free PowerPoint game templates, such as *Jeopardy*, *Who Wants to Be a Millionaire*, and *Are You Smarter than a 5th Grader?*

2. Click on the PowerPoint Game template you want to use. A pop-up window will ask if you want to Open the file or Save it. Click on Save.

3. The next window that opens will ask you where on your computer you want to save the template. Select a folder then click on Open. The template is now saved in a folder on your computer.

4. Arrange students into small groups. Explain that each group will create its own game as a way to review the information the students have been learning.

5. Make sure students are familiar with the format of the game they'll be creating, because they'll need to write their questions and answers in the same format.

6. For example, if students are writing questions for the Millionaire game, they'll need to write 15 questions, each one progressively more difficult. Each question will require four multiple choice answer options.

7. Before working on the computers give students time to plan and write out their questions on paper.

8. When students are ready to work on the computer, have them open the folder where you saved the game and click on the template to open it. Creating the game is simple. Students just need to type their questions and answers onto each of the slides.

9. Remind students to continually save their work. The first time they save their game, they'll need to go to File, click on Save As, and name the game.

10. Allow groups time to present their games to the class or make all of the games available on the computer in your classroom or computer lab. Students can play them to review for a test. You can also save the PowerPoint games to your authorSTREAM account so students can have access to them at home.

Get Real

Once you have your authorSTREAM account created, you can quickly and easily upload presentations. If you want to post student work, I suggest having an account for each class or hour. Do make your authorSTREAM web address available to your students and parents so they can access it often. All of your presentations will be on your page, and this will be very helpful to others.

Even if you've never narrated a PowerPoint presentation, consider recording your students or yourself and saving that as part of your presentation. This provides your audience with not only the visual, but more details through the audio. To record using PowerPoint, look under the Slideshow heading and click on Record Narration. This will allow you to record on one slide, or throughout the entire presentation. If your computer does not have an external microphone, you'll need to purchase an inexpensive microphone or borrow one from your school's technician.

> Digital technology gives everyone the means to express themselves, and it empowers them to speak—and to be heard by others, including those in power—in ways that previous generations could only have imagined.
>
> —JOHN PALFREY AND URS GASSER (2008)

There are many versions of Power-Point. If you have the 2007 version at home and the school still has the 2000 version, make sure to save your work as the 97–2003 version at home. Then when you get to school, you'll still be able to view the presentation. If you save it as a 2007 version and you don't have that version on your computer at school, it won't open and you'll be very frustrated. Also, if students are working on a Power-Point presentation at home, remind them to save it in the correct format so it can be viewed at school.

You can find many PowerPoint presentations already created by teachers on Pete's PowerPoint Station at http://pppst.com/. You can preview the lessons and then save them to your computer to use later. You can even edit them to fit your curriculum. It's a wonderful resource that'll save you lots of time!

Live Binders

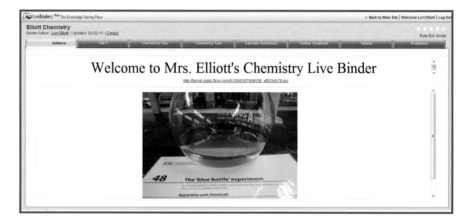

If you're like me, then throughout your teaching career you've accumulated a vast number of 3-ring binders. These notebooks are filled with lesson plans, professional development materials, curriculum, and so on. I remember when they invented the clear sleeve on the cover of binders. Man, that was cool. I could create my cutesy cover sheet and slide it right into my binder. I would show up at faculty meetings looking like I had my act together. Well, take the concept of the 3-ring binder and push it into the digital age. What you get is an online tool called Live Binders.

Live Binders is a free online tool that helps you create the digital equivalent of the traditional 3-ring binder. You can fill your binder with favorite websites, documents, images, and videos. Think of all the things you'd have traditionally put in a 3-ring binder. Now you can organize those items online and share them. You can create a Live Binder for a famous person, a favorite author, a reading skill, a time period in history, or an entire subject area such as biology. You can create a binder that functions as a back-to-school resource for parents or one that's full of educational games. Students, parents, and colleagues can access your notebook and get the resources they need at any time of the day or night.

Let's say you're putting together an author unit on Jan Brett. You can create a Live Binder filled with links to the author's website, reading log documents that you've created, and activities that go with each of her books.

What if you teach high school chemistry? Put together a Chemistry Live Binder for your students. Include your class syllabus, video clips of experiments, links to the online textbook your school uses, and copies of notes for the semester. If you were a student, wouldn't you like to click on a button and get all that information? If you're collaborating with other teachers, wouldn't sharing your binders lessen everyone's workload?

Now What?

One great thing about Live Binders is that you can set up an account for free. Are you ready to get organized?

SET UP AN ACCOUNT

1. Go to Live Binders at http://livebinders.com/. Look at the top right-hand corner for the Sign Up button. Click on Sign Up to begin.

2. Complete the account information and click on Sign Up when you're finished.

3. When you've completed the registration, a new screen will appear. You can either jump right into creating your first binder or you can choose to install a Live Binder It icon onto your computer's toolbar.

GET YOURSELF AN ICON

Let's tackle adding the Live Binder It icon to your toolbar. It allows you to save favorite websites immediately to your Live Binders. I think you'll enjoy using it, and it'll reduce your workload in the long run. You may need your school's technician to help you with this step because you probably don't have permission to download a program onto your school computer.

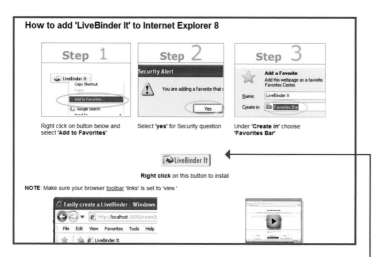

1. Scroll down the page a little bit until you see the steps to adding the Live Binder It tool. In the middle of the page you'll see a Live Binder It button. Underneath the button it says, right click on this button to install.

2. After you right click, (if you have a one-button mouse, hold down the control key and click), you'll see a menu. Click on Add to Favorites. A security alert will pop up just to make sure you want to add it to your computer. Click on Yes.

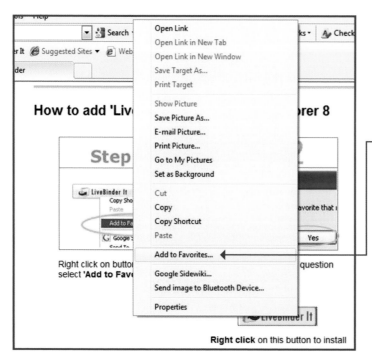

3. A new window will pop up that says Add a Favorite. You'll want to click on the icon next to Favorites to reveal the pull-down menu. Click on the Favorites Bar so that it's highlighted. Now click on the Add button.

4. Look at the toolbar on the top of your screen. You should see the Live Binder It icon. Now, when you're looking at a website and think you want to save it in a binder, you'll just click on that icon.

MAKE A NEW BINDER

1. To make a new binder, go to the Live Binder home page and click on the tab labeled Create Binder. When the new screen appears, click on the Start a Blank Binder option listed on the top of the page.

2. Here you'll be prompted to type in the title of your binder, a description of its contents, and word tags that might help others find it in a search. You'll also need to choose to make your binder public or private.

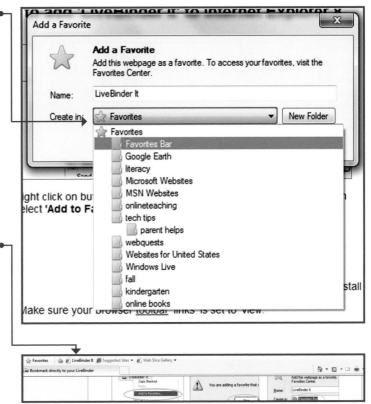

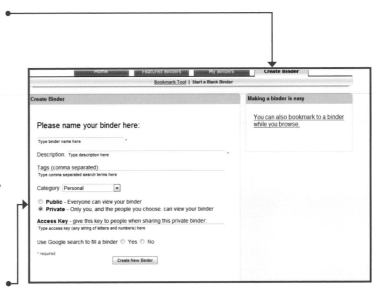

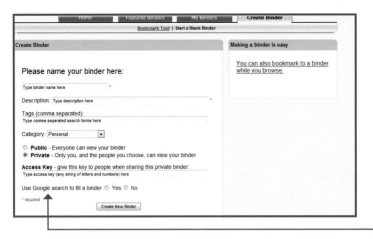

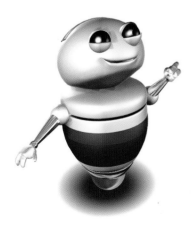

3. Public means anyone can view it and it'll be posted in the Live Binder Gallery. Private means only people you invite may view it. Your guests will need a special Access Key to view a Private binder. You'll create the Access Key right here.

4. If you'd like to gather resources quickly, you may want to select the Google Search option. Type in the topic of your binder and Live Binders will search Google and place the results immediately in your binder. You'll want to check those resources and delete any that are unwanted.

5. Click on Create New Binder. The next screen that appears is your brand new empty binder. (Of course, if you selected the Google Search option your binder will not be empty.) Now it's time for the fun part—creating your tabs!

LABEL YOUR TABS

1. A tab represents one page in your binder. A subtab is a resource that gets listed on a page. Decide how many tabs you'll need. You can always add a new tab or delete one later if you choose.

2. At the very top where you see Tab 1, click on the icon of the arrow. A small window will open. This is where you click to add, move, and delete tabs and subtabs. The arrow icon always appears on the tab you've selected. This allows you to work with each tab individually.

3. To name a tab, click on the tab until the text is highlighted in blue then type in your label.

ADD TO THAT BINDER

1. To add a website to a tab, paste or type the address of the website in the yellow box; then click on Insert. You'll see the website displayed on the tab you selected.

2. If you want more than one website to appear in this tab, click on New Subtab. Add the new web address, and click on Insert. You'll notice

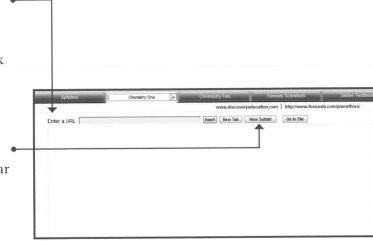

that each website address appears written in blue text on the top of your page.

3. Binders aren't just for websites. You can fill your binder with documents and pictures from your computer, or images from Flickr, and videos from YouTube™.

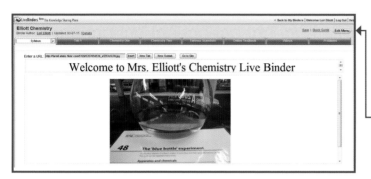

4. Click on the yellow Edit Menu button on the upper right-hand side of the screen to reveal the Edit Menu. A new set of tools will appear at the bottom of the screen.

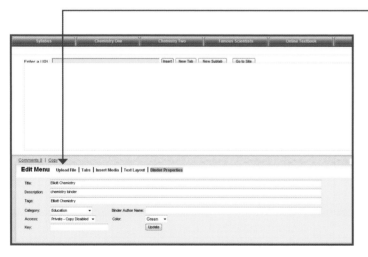

5. To place a document or picture you've saved on your computer into your binder, click Upload File. The first step is to select your file. To do that, click on Browse. A pop-up screen will appear. Use the drop-down menu at the top of this screen to locate your file.

6. For instance, if you saved a file to My Documents, click on My Documents. That will display all of the items you've saved there. Scroll through the list until you find the one you want. Click on it to select it, and then click on the Open button.

7. To insert pictures from Flickr or videos from YouTube™, click on Insert Media. Type what you're looking for in the search bar, and then click on Find. Scan through your options by clicking on the blue arrows. To select a picture or video, you just click on it.

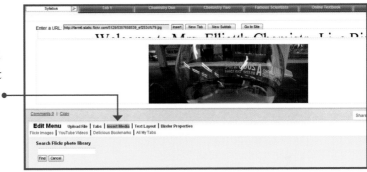

8. Click on the Text Layout button. You'll find templates that allow you to design the look of each page in your binder. I really like this option because it helps to give your binder an organized look and feel.

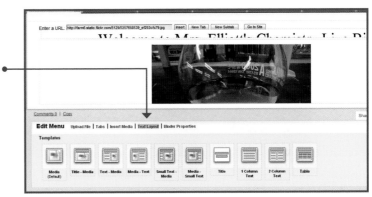

9. To add a picture to the cover of your binder and to choose the background color for your binder pages, click on Binder Properties. Here you can also add to or change your original binder settings.

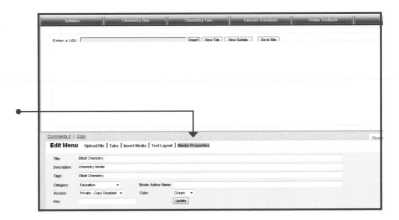

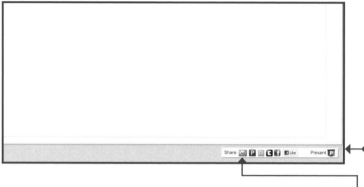

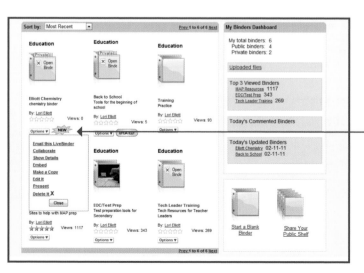

SHARE YOUR BINDER

1. The final step is to share your Live Binder with your students and their families or your colleagues.

2. Scroll down to the bottom of the page. Find the Share menu bar. It has icons such as an envelope, the Twitter logo, and the Facebook logo.

3. To e-mail your binder, click on the icon of the envelope. A screen will pop up allowing you to invite others to view your binder. If you made your binder Private, don't forget to include in your message the Access Key you created.

4. If you click on one of the other icons, such as Twitter or Facebook, Live Binders will automatically post your binder to your account on that site.

5. Here's another way you can share your binder. Go to the top of the page and click on My Binders. You'll see all of your binders with an Options tool displayed under each one. Click on Options to open a menu of choices.

6. I want to point out the Collaborate option. Not only does this allow you to share the binder with colleagues, but it lets you give them permission to add to the binder. It really is just like passing around your 3-ring notebook for others to use!

Let Me Show You

LESSON Student Research

Good teaching involves great preparation. Provide your students with a binder full of the tools they'll need to be successful for a unit of study, an entire subject area, or a course. Planning ahead saves time and frustration in the end.

1. Prior to assigning a student research project, search for helpful websites for the selected topics. Place needed rubrics, requirement sheets, graphic organizers, and actual websites in a Live Binder.

2. Consider labeling each tab with a title that helps students move through the research process in order. For example, if the research is about a country, you might label the tabs: Project Information, Location, Climate, Animals, Plants, and Culture.

3. The key to using Live Binders successfully is to make sure your audience knows where to find your binder. Make the binder accessible to students and their families. Publicize it in all of your communications—your class newsletter, website, blog, and syllabus.

4. Students will use the graphic organizer you provided to gather information from the resources you have put in your Live Binder.

5. You can even display final student work on the final tab of the Live Binder when the project has been completed.

Get Real

Pop-up blockers can get in the way of using some great tools. But have no fear; you can just turn them off if you're facing that challenge. Usually with pop-up blockers, a bar will appear at the top of your screen with a warning message. You'll want to select Always

> What the most effective teachers have discovered . . . is that good tools can make learning more efficient. New technologies make it possible for learners to sift through information quickly, collaborate on shared content easily, and reach influential audiences with little effort.
>
> —WILLIAM FERRITER (2009)

Allow Pop Ups from Live Binders. If the bar does not appear, look at your icons on the top of your screen. You may have an icon with a big, red crash on it. Click on this and select Allow Pop Ups.

Many schools don't allow or give you access to download things onto school computers which means you won't be able to put the Live Binder It icon on your desktop. Don't worry. You don't need the Live Binder It icon to use the tool. Just skip that step and copy and paste the website's address onto your binder pages instead.

A really helpful feature of Live Binders is the Featured Binders section. Here you can view other binders created by teachers or other people. Search the education section and you'll find hundreds of resources already organized for you or your students to use. If a binder is public, use it. Why spend time doing something that's already been done?

Blogs

Communicating with students and parents is something I've always worked really hard at throughout my career as a teacher. Time spent building and maintaining lines of communication is time well spent. In the old days, I'd type my newsletters and memos on brightly colored paper and place them in backpacks, just hoping they'd make it home and parents would retrieve them. The reality was, and still is, that the backpack method of communication is hardly a reliable one.

Back then, I couldn't have imagined all the different methods of communication available today. E-mail, social networking, a school website, and an online grading system are just a few of the digital tools I, and thousands of other teachers, use to get the news out about events, grades, and learning. Yet, perhaps my favorite digital tool for communicating is the blog. I love blogs. I have a number of blogs, each for a different purpose and audience. They're free, easy to update, and can be as playful or professional as your personality allows.

Maybe you aren't familiar with blogs. A blog, which is a mix of the words "web" and "log," is a website that posts information in reverse chronological order. The newest post appears at the top of the screen with the earlier posts following below. It's an ideal communication tool for teachers. But it's also a powerful learning tool. You see, a blog isn't just a place to post information; it's interactive. It allows readers to comment on the posts and to share their thoughts and ideas. It's a place where students can be asked to respond to prompts or questions about content. I use blogs to conduct book discussions, chronicle science experiments, and create simulations of historical events. I've even asked students to create their own blogs to reflect on their learning.

Now What?

There are many free sites that you can use to create your own blog. I personally use Blogger. I've used it for years without any problems or worries. It's not an education blog, but it works well for my purposes. Setting up a blog takes just a few steps and just a few minutes. If you don't already have a Gmail account created through Google, you'll need to do that first.

CREATE YOUR BLOG

1. Go to Blogger at http://www.blogger.com/. Click on the button that says Get Started to create a Gmail account. If you already have a Gmail account, just sign in.

2. Now click on Create a Blog. You'll be prompted to give your blog a title and an address. Try to make them match if possible. It will be easier for readers to remember the address that way.

3. To find out if the address you want to use is available, click on Check Availability. Before clicking on Continue, you'll need to type those squiggly letters into the box provided in the Word Verification section as a security measure.

4. Select the template you want for your blog. This is the background and layout. You can always go back and change this, so don't worry if you aren't thrilled about it. Click on the template you want, and then click on Continue.

5. You're done. Can you believe it? You now have a blog of your own. Click on the Start Blogging button. This is where you'll write your posts, or entries. Each time you want to post something, you'll log in to your Blogger account and click on New Post.

SELECT SECURITY SETTINGS

I bet you're excited to begin, but before you start posting, I want to make

sure you know how to control the security settings. That way you can rest assured that your blog is safe for you and your students to use. Of course you should check with your school about their policies regarding blogs and follow any regulations concerning posting information and student images or work.

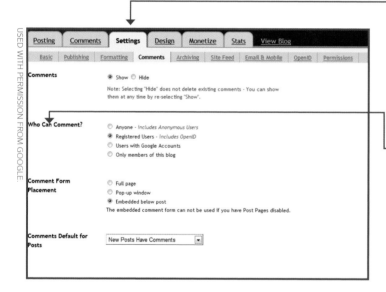

1. Look at the top of the posting screen. Click on the Settings button. Scan across the top. See all of the subheads written in blue? Click on the Comments button.

2. Under Who Can Comment, I always select Anyone. That's because I don't want my students to need an e-mail account in order to post to my blog.

3. Since this choice allows anyone to anonymously post to my blog, I assign each of my students a code name or number. They use their code names to identify themselves at the end of their comments instead of using their real names.

4. Scroll down the page to Comment Moderation. I select the Always option. That way, I can see everything people write before it goes on the blog. If for some reason I don't like a comment, I can simply reject it.

5. If you choose Comment Moderation, type in your e-mail address. That way the comments will be sent to your e-mail too.

6. Scroll down the page again. Under Show Word Verification, I recommend selecting the Yes option because that prevents spam from getting on your blog.

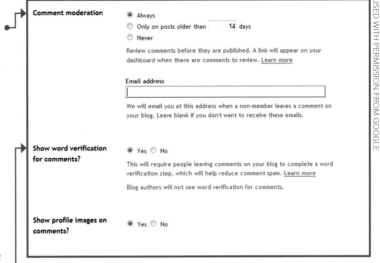

START BLOGGING

1. To get back to your new post, click on the Posting tab. The screen that pops up may look familiar to you. You'll find the tools there are just like those found in Word or other word processing programs.

2. Make sure you're on the Compose tab to write, post pictures, post videos, and add links to websites.

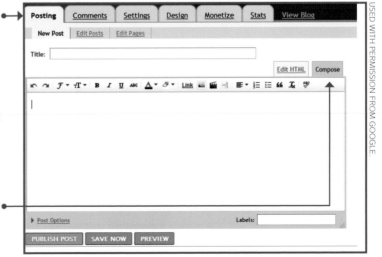

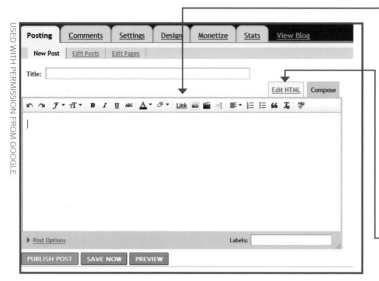

3. To post a link to a website, click on the Link button. A small pop-up window will open. Type or copy and paste the URL from the website into the space provided. Click OK; then click Publish Post. Now when people click on that link, they'll go to that website.

4. To embed html code, make sure you're on the Edit html tab. To embed means to place something, such as a website or online video, right there on the page for others to view.

5. To embed let's say a Teacher Tube video, copy the embed code provided by the site for your video. This is not just the URL or website's address. In fact it's a rather long stream of letters and symbols. On any video site or picture slideshow site, the Embed code is usually provided. Simply copy that long code and paste it into the box here. Click on Publish Post. That's all there is to it!

Let Me Show You

LESSON Hitch Your Wagons!

Create a blog for a social studies topic such as westward expansion. Students must visit the blog each day to learn their Assignment of the Day. Students love this! Along the way they respond to prompts and questions, take online assessments, and chronicle and reflect on their learning.

Here are a few highlights from the westward expansion unit I've taught using a blog.

1. Day 1: Students visit the blog and take an online quiz about the Louisiana Purchase. This is a great way to assess students' prior knowledge on this topic.

2. Day 4: Students refer to the blog to find all of the directions and resources they'll need to complete a project about Lewis and Clark.

3. Day 8: Students read the blog to learn the names of actual pioneer families, their occupations, and their reasons for heading west. Student groups must choose a name for their family and work together to create a detailed description of their family based on their research. Each group uses the comment section on the blog to record their family's history.

4. Day 10: The blog provides information and links about the supplies needed to travel west. The pioneer families access those materials from the blog and "pack their wagons." Students are responsible for posting comments on the blog that explain what they chose to bring and why.

5. Days 13–18: Pioneer families face a new challenge each day. The blog presents the challenge through video clips you post. Families must each decide their own fate. What choices will they make? Their decisions and highlights of their discussion are recorded on the blog.

6. Day 25: As the unit of westward expansion comes to a close, pictures and video of the culminating Pioneer Day event are posted so friends and families can enjoy the celebration of learning.

Get Real

Right off the bat I need to let you know that some school districts block access to blogs. Even though I think they are safer than many other online sites, many districts are concerned about students viewing inappropriate material. Often, explaining to the person in charge of your filter the reasons why you want access to a certain site will get it opened.

If blogs are blocked in your district, you may instead want to use a website such as Weebly at http://www.weebly.com/ to make your own webpage.

Be aware that Blogger is not an education site. If students click on the Next Blog button they may end up where you don't want them to go. There's a way to remove this option. Visit the following site for more details: http://www.mydigitallife.info/2009/01/12/how-to-remove-and-hide-blogger-nav-bar-top-navigation-bar/.

You can allow only an invited group of people to access your blog on Blogger. To do this, click on the Settings tab, and

> The Internet is no longer simply a place where digital learners consume information. It is now also a forum through which users can publish and broadcast their own writing.
>
> —WILL RICHARDSON (2006)

then click on the Permissions button. Under the heading Blog Readers, select the Only People I Choose option. You'll need to type in the e-mail addresses of your readers, and they'll have to log in with a username and password each time they want to see your blog.

To get parents and students familiar with your blog, always place your blog address on all of your other forms of communication. Send the link in e-mails to parents. Challenge students to be the first to comment on a post and offer a prize.

Make your blog one that readers want to return to often to see new things. If you create a blog and rarely update it, then students and parents won't take time to visit. If updating your blog becomes part of your daily or weekly routine, then your audience will grow.

Other popular blog sites include Edublogs at http://edublogs.org/ and WordPress at http://wordpress.org/.

Edmodo

Have you "friended" your classmates from back in junior high? Have you connected with folks who wouldn't speak to you in high school but now want your help with their Farmville requests? Have you updated your status with news of your latest shopping finds? If you answered yes to any of those questions, then you're a Facebooker.

If you don't know what I'm talking about, then welcome to the world of social networking. Social networking has become the way people communicate with each other. I enjoy using social networking sites of all kinds. I tweet on Twitter. I post to walls of friends on Facebook. I share the novel I'm reading on Shelfari. Even young kids are chatting with each other online at WebKinz and Club Penguin.

I've seen the benefits of communicating in this new format. Students ask questions and make positive comments about the activities in the classroom; they even share online resources. But, of course, there are always concerns. Everyone's heard the horror stories that involve some type of cyber bullying or the inappropriate use of a social networking site. While I don't think banning social networking use is the answer, I do think we need to educate and monitor student and adult use. I tell my own children, my students, and all of the teachers I train, "Don't put anything on the web that you wouldn't be comfortable posting on the front page of your local newspaper."

When you post to the web you're putting images, words, and information out there that can impact your future.

Can such a popular tool be used in the classroom? Thanks to Edmodo, the answer is yes. It's really revolutionized communication for thousands of teachers and students. Edmodo is an educational version of Facebook. It looks like it; it works like it; but it provides more security and focuses on education. Edmodo is unlike other social networking sites because students cannot just randomly find other students. They must have a purpose for being there. They must be assigned to a Group and without the code, they can't join a group.

With Edmodo you can post assignments and discussion questions, send alerts about upcoming events or tests, or upload a practice math sheet or links to helpful websites. You can even place videos on your page for students to view. Edmodo is just what the iGeneration of learners and teachers have been looking for.

Now What?

Registering for an account on Edmodo is free and takes just a minute or two.

GET REGISTERED

1. Visit Edmodo, http://www.edmodo.com/. There are three ways to register: As a Student, As a Teacher, or As a Parent. You must register first, before your students and their parents can register.

2. Click on I'm a Teacher. You'll need to fill in the information including your e-mail address and then click on Sign Up. Now lickety split your page will pop up. It's that easy to get started.

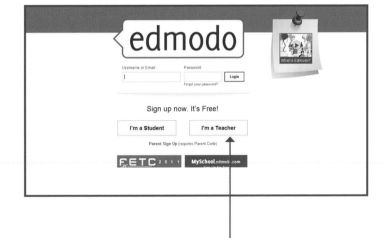

SET UP GROUPS

1. Now you'll set up your classes. Edmodo calls these groups. Think about the groups you want to establish.

2. If you're an elementary teacher, maybe you just want a "Mrs. Elliott's Class" group. If you're a secondary teacher, you might want to set up groups such as "Elliott English 1" and "Elliott English 2."

3. Creating multiple groups helps you manage the pages and gives you the flexibility to post information that's specific to each group. Remember, if you're going to include parents, you'll need to set up a Parent Group too.

4. To add a group, look on the left–hand side of the screen under the icon of the person. Find and click on the word Create. A pop-up window will open. You'll need to give your group a name and assign it a grade level and subject area.

5. When you're done, a new pop up, this one containing a code, will appear on the screen. This is really important. It contains the code the students need in order to register and join your group. This is a wonderful security feature.

6. Instruct students and parents to go to http://www.edmodo.com/ and register. Provide them with their code and have them join your group.

START POSTING

1. Now that you've set up your groups and students and parents have joined, what will you do with Edmodo? Look at your menu of choices in the rectangular box at the top of the screen.

2. You can send a note. Click on the Note icon of the notepad and type your message in the text box.

3. You can click on the Alert icon to announce or remind the group members of a special date, upcoming fieldtrip, or event.

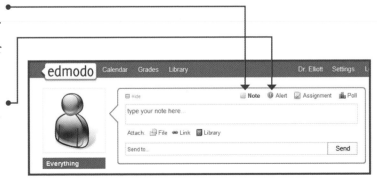

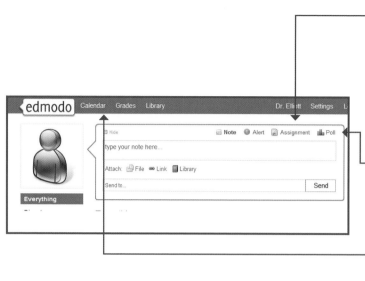

4. You can post an Assignment, and the group members can actually turn it in on Edmodo. The students' work is private and goes directly to the teacher.

5. You can also set up a poll to get responses about a question by clicking on the Poll icon.

6. Notice at the very top of your Edmodo page you can set up a calendar or even a grade book if you want to provide that for parents.

ATTACH, LINK, AND EMBED MATERIAL

1. When you send a note or an assignment, you'll see that you have an Attach option with three choices: File, Link, and Library.

2. Your Library is empty now, but as you put files and links on Edmodo, they'll be saved there. Students or parents can search the library to find the files you've posted.

3. Let's say you get near the end of the quarter and a student has missed an assignment. Parents and students can search the Library and easily find the needed assignment, complete it, and turn it in before the deadline.

4. To place a document or picture from your computer on Edmodo, click on Attach File. A pop-up window will open. You'll need to browse or look for the file on your computer, click on it to select it, and then click on Open.

5. Your document is now on Edmodo for your students and/or parents to access. This is a great way to post field trip forms, review notes, or even a practice math sheet.

6. Click on Attach Link to share the link to a website or to embed a video, slideshow, or other multimedia product. All you'll need to do to link a website is either type or copy and paste the URL or web address from the website and paste it here.

7. To embed means to place a video, slideshow, or other multimedia product right there on the page to view immediately, rather than clicking on a link to get there.

8. To embed let's say a Brain Pop video, you'll copy the embed code provided by the site for your video. Most multimedia sites usually provide the URL and the embed code. Simply copy that long stream of letters and symbols and paste it in the box here on the Attach Link section of Edmodo.

Let Me Show You

LESSON Literature Group Discussions

Engage your readers in online book discussions by using Edmodo.

1. Use Edmodo to facilitate an online book discussion about the novel being read in class. Pose a question and ask students to respond by replying to the question.

2. Continue the discussion by linking a graphic organizer, such as a story map, for students to use to complete homework.

3. Another day, embed a video clip of an interview with the book's author. Have students comment on what they learned from the interview and what purpose the author might have had for writing this book.

4. Post an assignment. Ask students to write a poem based on the character traits of the main character and turn it in on Edmodo.

5. Create a poll asking students which of the posted events might happen at the end of the book. Have students vote using the poll and then discuss the reasons for each prediction.

6. Ask students to post their critique of the novel at the end of the unit. Who would they recommend the book to and what did they like best about the book?

Get Real

Social networking can be a sticky subject in some districts. Do check with your administrator or school handbook to make sure the use of Edmodo is allowed. Educate school leaders that this is an educational site and it's secure. Students can't post pictures or find other students outside of their group. The focus of all discussion should be educational and appropriate.

Edmodo works best when we actively use it, just like Facebook. If rarely anything is posted, then students won't visit there often. In fact, they'll stay on the social networking sites where the action is! So, keep the conversation moving.

Obviously, student access to computers is necessary for this kind of tool to be useful. For those without computer access at home, make sure the computer in the classroom is available or time in the computer lab is provided so everyone can participate in the discussions.

You're the boss! Establish clear guidelines for student behavior on Edmodo. Students should not reveal their personal information or use inappropriate language. They should not say negative things about students or teachers. You are in control of every message, and you can remove any comment. You can also remove a student from the group. Hover to the right of the post or comment and three icons will appear to allow you to Remove, Edit, or Enlarge the comment.

> Technology is all about engagement. Watching the intense looks on our children's and teens' faces as they play video games, text all day long, Skype, Facebook, watch YouTube videos, and juggle a dozen websites at a time, we can clearly see that they are engaged.
>
> —LARRY ROSEN (2010)

Wallwisher

Some inventions just make our lives so much easier. Where would we be without the flat iron to smooth our untamed hair or the coffee maker that turns on while we sleep? Sticky notes are definitely one of the handiest inventions I use. I have sticky notes in all sorts of colors, sizes, and shapes. I use them to remind me of everything from getting magazines when I go to the store to what time I need to pick up my daughter from play practice. They've revolutionized teaching. Seriously. I don't know of a teacher who doesn't ask students to place sticky notes in the books they're reading, or to respond to a question by writing on a sticky note that gets posted on the board.

Well, believe it or not, sticky notes have gone digital. Wallwisher has taken the idea of the paper notes and put them online. Now you can create a wall on which your students can post their thoughts, comments, questions, or ideas.

Now What?

Setting up a wall is quick and easy. I'll walk you through the steps. Just take a minute to come up with a question or thought that you'd like to post on your wall.

BUILD A WALL

1. Go to Wallwisher at http://www.wallwisher. com/. You can register for an account first, which is free, or you can just start building a wall and then register later.

2. To start building a wall, scroll across the top of the homepage and click on Build a Wall. You should see several boxes on the screen. Let's work through them one at a time.

3. At the top, on the left-hand side is a small box that says Click to Select Image. By click-ing on this box, you'll be able to choose a picture to represent the idea on your wall.

4. Click on one of the images provided, or click Browse to upload a picture from your computer. The image from your computer must be a very small size, no bigger than 512 kb, so you may want to use one of the options provided.

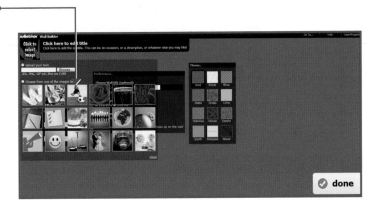

5. Once you've selected an image, look at the bot-tom right-hand corner of the box and click on the Close button. This takes you back to the main screen.

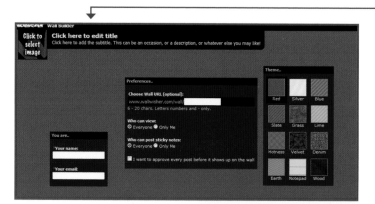

6. Look to the right of the image you just loaded and find the box that says Click Here to Edit Title and Click Here to Add the Subtitle. Click on the words and type in your title and subtitle.

CHOOSE PREFERENCES

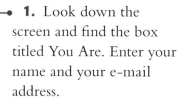

1. Look down the screen and find the box titled You Are. Enter your name and your e-mail address.

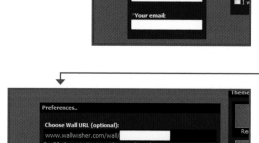

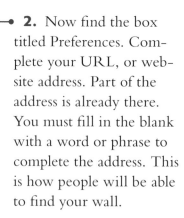

2. Now find the box titled Preferences. Complete your URL, or website address. Part of the address is already there. You must fill in the blank with a word or phrase to complete the address. This is how people will be able to find your wall.

3. The next step is to decide who can view and post to your wall. Your choices are Everyone or Only Me.

4. In order to control the content that appears on your wall, I recommend you check the box that says, "I want to approve every post before it shows up on the wall."

5. The farthest box to the right, titled Theme, offers you several options for the background of your wall. Click on the design that you like best. Then click on Done. Once you select Done, your wall is built and will appear on the screen.

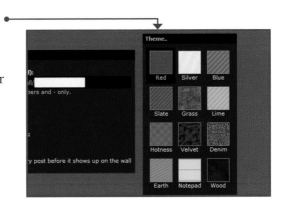

SHARE YOUR WALL

1. Now you can share your wall with others. Provide students, parents, or colleagues with the URL. Look at the top of the page. You'll see that the website address there is the one you created earlier.

2. If you have a website or blog, click on the Do More button to find the embedding code you'll need to post your wall to those places. (To learn how to embed to a blog, see page 134.)

Let Me Show You

LESSON 1 Get into the Book

Have students make predictions about the book the class is reading and then post their predictions to Wallwisher using digital sticky notes.

1. Create a Wallwisher with a question such as, "What do you think will happen in Chapter 5?" Provide your students with the Wallwisher address. If you have an existing class website, be sure to post the Wallwisher address there too.

2. A day or two later, show the Wallwisher to the class and discuss the predictions they made. Move the notes around to create categories and compare common answers.

LESSON **2** Student of the Week

Build a sense of community in your class by celebrating a different student each week!

1. Select a student of the week. Create a Wallwisher page that features the student. Upload an image of the student or use an image of something she enjoys.

2. At the beginning of the week, during announcements or Morning Meeting, show the Wallwisher to the class. Invite them to post notes that compliment the student or describe her best qualities.

3. Share the Wallwisher website address with students, parents, and teachers.

4. At the end of the week, share the Wallwisher with the class again. Send the link containing the wall to the student's e-mail account or her parents' e-mail.

LESSON **3** Homework Helper

Provide your students with a place to view their homework assignments and post any questions they may have about them.

1. Create a Homework Helper Wallwisher. Post homework assignments on your wall. Encourage students to post any questions or confusions they experience with their homework or current assignments.

2. Share the website address with your students and their parents. To respond to the questions on the Homework Helper, you can post responses, or post a note that you'll go over the questions in class the next day.

3. Since students don't need to register for an account to comment on Wallwisher, they don't have to worry about others "finding out" that they don't understand an assignment. Getting this type of honest feedback will help you to know where to take your instruction next.

Get Real

The only real obstacle of this simple and easy-to-use tool is access. It works best when students have access to the Internet either at school or at home. If you have a computer lab, allow students time to work on the Wallwisher parts of their assignments when your class visits the lab. Or, display the Wallwisher at the beginning of class and as attendance and preliminary class routines are taking place, have students use the computer to post their ideas.

> Kids who have grown up digital expect to talk back, to have conversation. They want choice in their education, in terms of what they learn, when they learn it, where, and how. They want their education to be relevant to the real world, the one they live in.
>
> —DON TAPSCOTT (2009)

If a student registers with Wallwisher, his username will appear on his comments, but if he doesn't register, the sticky notes will be posted anonymously. Anonymity can help motivate students to share their true thoughts and feelings, but it can also provide an opportunity for negative responses. When you set up a wall, remember to select the option that says, "I want to approve every post before it shows up on the wall." That way you can monitor the comments, especially if you're using a wall to discuss a class issue or recognize a student.

Glogster

Take a walk around just about any school and check out the student work on display. I bet you'll see lots of posters. Posters are a very visual and creative way for students to demonstrate their learning. We have kids make posters with timelines and Venn diagrams. We have them make posters of themselves, famous people, and community helpers. I especially love the "Vote for Joe, He's in the Know" and "Go Green" versions of posters. Posters can be made very inexpensively. Just grab a poster board, some markers, maybe a little glitter. You're good to go.

But what if students could take the content they've learned and display their posters online for a larger audience? What if students could insert video clips, sound, and website links so the reader could interact with the information? Sound like an interesting possibility?

Meet Glogster, a free online tool that allows students and teachers to create online multimedia posters called glogs. A glog can include text, pictures, video, sound, links, and colorful backgrounds, all of which make reading them very interesting. So, come on. Put those markers aside and try making a poster the Glogster way.

Now What?

Glogster wasn't originally intended to be an education tool, but because of its popularity with teachers and students, the makers of Glogster developed Glogster EDU, giving students a private and safe environment in which to work. You can register for a free basic Glogster EDU account or subscribe for a premium account.

REGISTER YOURSELF AND YOUR CLASS

1. Go to Glogster at http://edu.glogster.com/. Click on EDU Basic. Complete the registration page. Once you click on Sign Up, a new screen appears.

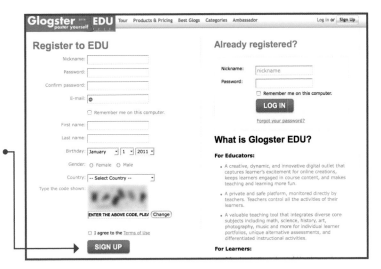

2. This new screen is called your Dashboard. To create accounts for your students, click on the Add New Students button.

3. A pop-up window will appear. Enter the number of students you want to add. The limit is 50. If you work with more than 50 students, you can always put students into groups and have them share the accounts.

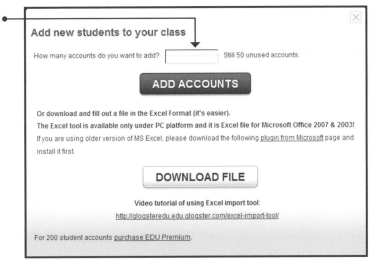

Glogster EDU subaccounts for nickname

01-29-2011 10:24

Glogster EDU subaccounts for nickname:

Your generated Student's accounts:

1. Nickname: setmpdv
   Password: mx7midpr
   First login link: http://edu.glogster.com/go/2q0kmc

2. Nickname: s4rfqqu
   Password: a37qbdq2
   First login link: http://edu.glogster.com/go/1oijlw

3. Nickname: s7cdusu
   Password: vfn2j2t9
   First login link: http://edu.glogster.com/go/63xchs

4. Nickname: shmby4q
   Password: 7x1z3wny
   First login link: http://edu.glogster.com/go/23gvpt

5. Nickname: sddf6xp
   Password: blnhewjl
   First login link: http://edu.glogster.com/go/6ng4pv

6. Nickname: sv7yax3
   Password: y4u2uepa
   First login link: http://edu.glogster.com/go/ghzxgk

7. Nickname: sv2qchd
   Password: jcvpd0n6
   First login link: http://edu.glogster.com/go/pqtp4i

4. Once you've added the number of students, look on your Dashboard for the Messages section. Glogster will have sent you a message containing the login information for your students.

5. Click on the message to see your students' passwords and login information. Print this page for your records, then click on Back to Dashboard.

6. You'll see your students' accounts on the dashboard page. Each one is represented by a picture of a teddy bear.

7. To edit an account, change a password, or delete a student, click on Manage Students in your Dashboard. It's a good idea to change the passwords to something everyone can remember instead of the random letters and numbers provided.

8. To change a password, click on the Change Password option under a teddy bear. When the pop-up screen appears, type in your new password and confirm it. You'll have to change each student's password individually.

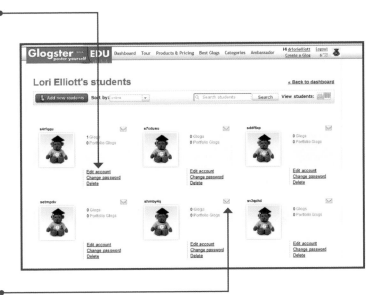

9. Notice the icon of an envelope by each of the student accounts. By clicking on that icon, you can send a student a message. This is a great way to easily post reminders or provide feedback.

READY, SET, GLOG!

1. Have students log in at http://edu.glogster.com/. Instruct each student to click on Log In and enter the username and password you provide. After students log in ask them to click on the pink Create a Glog button.

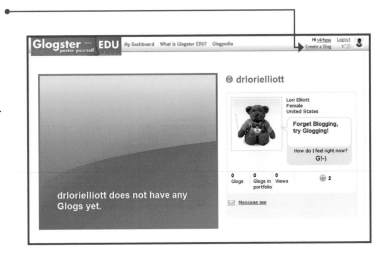

2. This is where the magic happens. Students use the tools on the toolbar to insert items such as graphics, text, and sound. Each time a category is selected a new window of options pops open. Students select what they

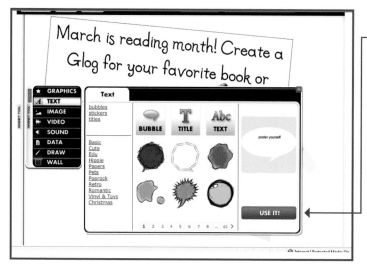

want to use and then click on the Use It button.

3. Any piece of the Glog can be moved around just by clicking and dragging. The best way to learn to Glog is to play around with it a bit.

SAVE AND SHARE THE GLOG

1. At the end of the work session, direct the students' attention to the text bar at the top of the screen. Instruct students to name their Glogs and then click the Save or Publish button. A new screen will pop up.

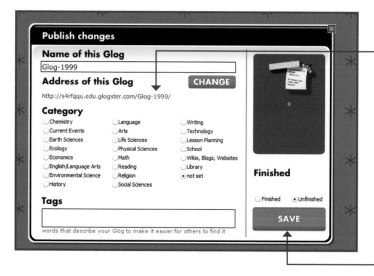

2. Here students can see the website address for their Glog. They can also select the category that best matches their Glog and type in tag words to help others locate their Glog in a search. In the box to the right, students check either finished or unfinished and then click on Save.

3. As the teacher, you're able to share students' completed Glogs in many different ways. Go back to your Dashboard. Under the pictures of the teddy bears is a section that says New Glogs from Class-mates. Click on the Glog you want to share.

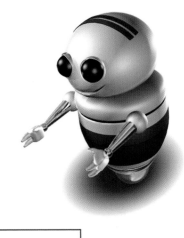

4. Once the Glog loads, scroll down the page and look to the right to see your options.

5. Click on the Embed button to get the Glog's URL or website address. Share this address on your own website or blog, or in a newsletter. To embed the Glog directly on your blog, copy the longer html code provided. Paste it into the html tab of your blog (see page 134 for embedding to a blog).

6. To send the Glog as an e-mail, click Send to Friends. To post it to your Edmodo account (see page 138), click on the Edmodo icon. To share a Glog with the entire class, click on the megaphone icon.

Let Me Show You

LESSON Newsletters

Students build and strengthen their interpersonal, organizational, note-taking, and writing skills as they work together to create an online classroom newsletter.

1. Organize the class into small groups of two or three. One group is selected each week to function as the classroom's news reporters. You might want to create and post a schedule so students will know when it'll be their turn.

2. The reporters are responsible for keeping notes about what is going on in the classroom and what they're learning about.

3. At the end of the week, perhaps during writing time, student reporters meet with you to present their plan for their Glog. Once you approve their plan, they can begin creating on Glogster.

4. Publish each week's Glog to your class website or blog for parents and students to view.

Get Real

Because Glogster is so much fun to use, it's imperative that students have a plan and complete all of their research before working at the computer. The Glog should showcase great learning, not just a flashy presentation.

The usernames and passwords provided by Glogster are clunky and hard to remember. Do change the passwords to something everyone can recall. Also, prepare an index card or printing label for each student with Glogster's URL and their username and password. Have students stick these on their notebooks or daily planners. It'll make it much easier for everyone!

> We teachers must begin by setting aside our traditional ideas of how things should be done in the classroom and accept that our students really have grown up on a different planet.
>
> —RICH ALLEN (2010)

Prezi

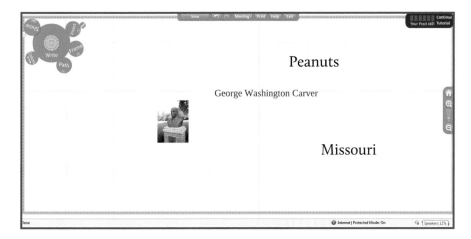

Over the years I've watched students of all ages jump right into a research topic and make it their own. They'll spend hours looking for information and talk to anyone who will listen to the amazing things they've discovered. The perfect ending to such an endeavor is to share a fabulous presentation with a real audience. PowerPoint is a wonderful tool to use and students are often very familiar with that format. But what if you have some students who want to spice things up a bit? Enter Prezi. I've often described it as PowerPoint on steroids!

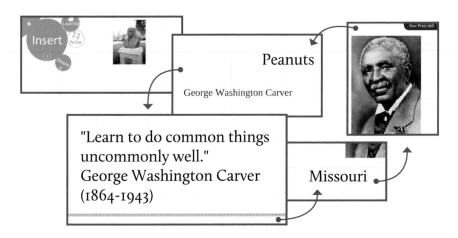

Prezi is an online presentation tool that takes the audience from idea to idea in a nonlinear fashion. Prezi is unique because you can design the presentation to move across the screen in any direction and zoom in and out on the information. This allows the presenter to focus on key words, phrases, or images and use movement to transition from idea to idea, which provides momentum. Imagine, after weeks of learning about George Washington Carver, how cool it would be to watch a presentation that could fly from a picture of George Washington Carver to a video clip of his home in Missouri and then zip to a famous quote that demonstrates his love of science.

What I like best about using Prezi with students is the fact that they can no longer simply paste in a list of bulleted ideas. Instead of slides, a Prezi actually starts with a blank canvas. Like an artist, the author of the Prezi chooses images, words, and video and then sets up the transitions from idea to idea. Prezi forces students to organize and prioritize information. Students must really understand their topic and then determine what the key words and images must be in order to convey that understanding.

When the presentations are given, there's no more reading from the slide, but rather a true discussion of the information. Also, because of the zooming and moving features, the audience is much more engaged in the presentation, and they tend to remember more of the information. Get ready to help students process information a little bit differently and present it in an exciting new way.

Now What?

Prezi offers a Teacher/Student account for free. Only current teachers and students can get an education account.

GET AN ACCOUNT

1. To set up a Prezi account for yourself or for your students, go to http://prezi.com/. Click on Sign Up Now.

2. You'll see a menu of Sign Up options. Go to the yellow Student/ Teacher Licenses box and click on the blue Go button.

3. The next page looks really similar to the one you just saw, but these are the Education choices. Click Get on the EDU Enjoy option.

4. A pop-up window opens to ask for your school e-mail. Prezi is looking for an educational institution's address. Many teachers use one e-mail address for an entire class and let each of the students in the class access that account.

5. If you want to create individual accounts for each student, but your students don't have school e-mail accounts, you can use Prezi without the EDU option. Sign up for the free Public account. That way you can use a basic Gmail or Yahoo account for your classes.

6. Once you enter your e-mail address click Continue. A pop-up window

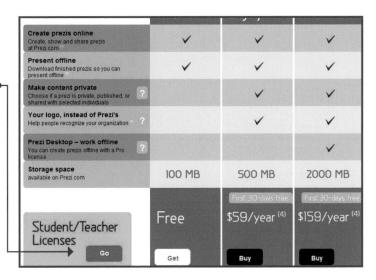

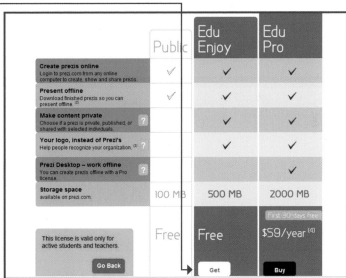

appears to tell you to check your e-mail account to verify the request. Go to your e-mail and click on the link provided in the message, which will take you back to the Prezi registration page.

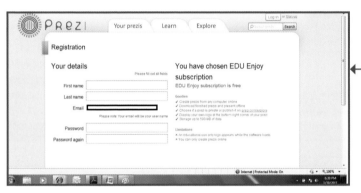

7. Fill in your information on the registration page. Your e-mail address will be your username. Check that you agree to the terms and then click on Done. You're now ready to create.

MAKE A PREZI

1. Click on the New Prezi button at the top left of the screen. A pop-up window opens. Fill in the title and a description of the Prezi you're about to create. Then click on New Prezi at the bottom of the screen.

2. You'll see a handy Prezi tutorial on the screen. I recommend taking a look at it to reinforce what's discussed here and to give you more confidence before placing items on the canvas. If you don't want to watch the tutorial or if you've seen it before, just click on the X in the corner of the tutorial and it'll go away.

3. This is your blank canvas. To insert text, click anywhere on the canvas and begin typing.

THE ZEBRA TOOL

1. The Zebra tool appears whenever you click on something that you've added to the canvas. The zebra looks like a blue circle made up of lines. It allows you to change the position, size, or orientation of text, frames, pictures, and videos—whatever you place on the canvas.

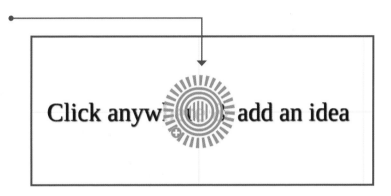

2. To move your selected item, click on the inner lines of the zebra and drag the item to where you want it.

3. To change the orientation of an item, click on the outer lines of the zebra and drag your mouse around in a circle. This allows you to create interesting effects such as making text look as if it's written upside down or on the diagonal.

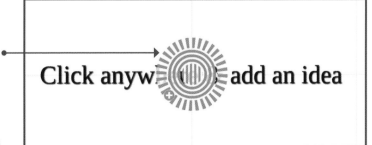

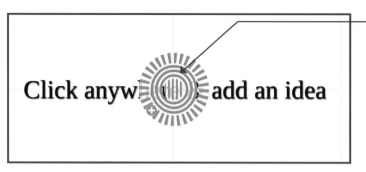

4. To make your selected item change in size, click and drag on the rings of the inner circle. Drag in to make the text or object smaller and drag out to make it larger.

THE BUBBLE TOOLS

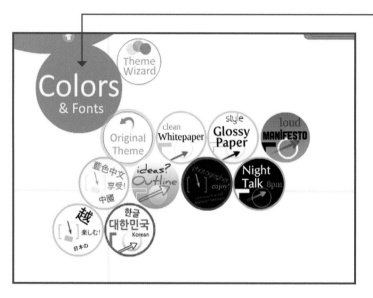

1. Look at the left-hand side of your canvas to find the tools you'll need to create a Prezi. Instead of a toolbar you have tool bubbles.

2. Click on the Colors and Fonts bubble to see options for your background color and text. There's even a Theme Wizard to guide you step-by-step through the creation. To get back to the tool bubble menu, click on the Arrow icon.

3. Try clicking on the Frame bubble. You'll want to use frames to organize your information. You can select frames that are visible or hidden. Framing information is helpful when you want to zoom in on a statement or picture.

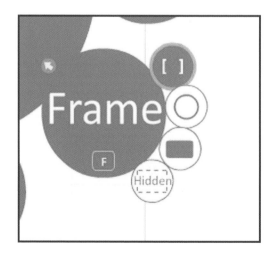

4. Prezi makes it easy to insert pictures, documents saved as PDF files, and videos. Click on the Insert tool bubble.

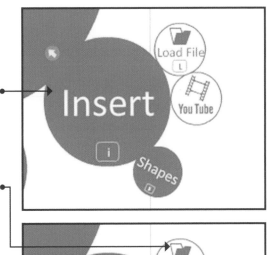

5. To insert a file, click on the bubble that says Load File. A pop-up window opens so you can browse your documents for the file you want to use. Click on the file and then click on Open. Your file is now on the Prezi canvas.

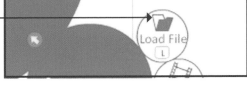

6. To insert a You-Tube™ video, click on the bubble labeled YouTube™. Copy the URL of the video you want and paste it in the space provided. To find the URL, look at the top of the YouTube™ webpage or next to the YouTube™ video.

7. To insert a shape, click on the Shape bubble. The shapes not only give a clean look to the presentation, but they can also be used as a way to organize a set of images and words.

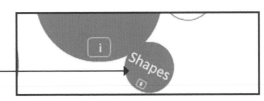

8. The next bubble on the tools is Path. This is a key feature. It's what you'll use to connect each

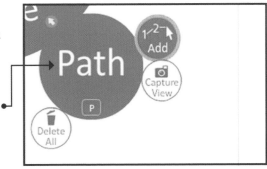

piece of information to the next. It works much like a dot-to-dot picture. Click on the first item to select it; then click on the next item you want to move to in your presentation.

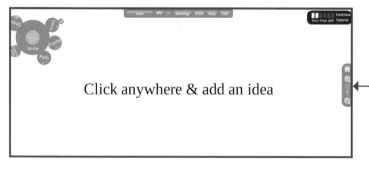

9. You can use the zoom bar on the right-hand side of the canvas to zoom in on information. Adding the path and zooming in create the movement the audience will experience during the presentation.

10. To view the presentation, click on the Show bubble. Click the arrows to make the presentation advance. When you're finished, click on the Back arrow of your Internet tool bar and click the Esc key to get out of full-screen mode.

SHARE YOUR PREZI

1. When you're finished with the Prezi, click on Exit. There's no Save button because your Prezi is constantly being saved while you work.

2. Once you click Exit, your Prezi will appear completed. To the right

of the screen are some tools. Here you can choose to edit, make a copy, or delete your Prezi.

3. Look below your Prezi to find options for sharing it. Click on Get Link to find the URL or website address for your Prezi. Share the URL in newsletters or on a class website or blog.

4. If you click on Embed, you'll be given a very long code that can be pasted on the html tab of a blog post or website. If you embed the Prezi to your blog, then the actual presentation and not just the link will appear on your blog.

5. Click on the icon of an Envelope to e-mail the Prezi.

6. Finally, make sure to select which security option you want. I recommend Private because only those you want to view the Prezi will have access, and others cannot download the students' work.

Let Me Show You

LESSON **1** Housing around the World

Students learn how climate drives the design and type of building materials used to build homes around the world. Then they display their findings in a dynamic Prezi presentation.

1. Prior to beginning the project, read aloud many picture books about different places in the world. Focus class discussion on the houses or living quarters in each country. Talk about why homes are built differently in each region.

2. Discuss how the weather and climate affect the type of housing and the kind of materials used to build the different homes in each region of the world.

3. Have students each draw one picture of a home. Be sure homes from many different regions are represented. Let students know that their pictures will be used to make a special presentation so they should try to include as much detail and color as possible in the drawings.

4. Scan the colorful pictures drawn by the students. Save the images to the computer, or computers, that your students will use to make their Prezis.

5. Have students work in teams of three. You'll want students who drew homes from very different regions to work together. Tell students that they'll create a Prezi about the different ways homes are made around the world.

6. Make sure each group completes a plan on paper before being allowed to work on the computer.

7. Each Prezi must feature the pictures of the homes students drew, as well as words that describe the materials necessary to make each type of house. Their presentations should also include information on the weather and climate in each region.

8. Once you've approved a group's plan, team members may work on the computer to create their Prezi.

9. Students should present their Prezis to classmates. You should also post them on the class blog, if you have one, for others to see.

LESSON 2 Decades of History

Students research the pop culture of a decade and then present their learning in a multimedia presentation using Prezi.

1. Begin with what students think they know about the decades spanning from the 1950s through to the 1990s. List pop culture icons, fashion, music, fads, and so on.

2. Show video clips of each decade to build more understanding. For tips on finding video clips, go to page 29.

3. Divide students into groups of two or three. Each group selects a decade to research in depth. You can divide the decades into categories or have more than one group work on the same decade. You may also want to include political events and natural disasters in addition to pop culture.

4. Provide students with a rubric and timeline for the project. Your rubric might include a certain number of facts, at least one video and four images, correct spelling, and accurate information presented.

5. You should also provide them with graphic organizers so they can record the information they find while researching.

6. After completing their research, students should outline their presentation before working on the computers to create the Prezi.

7. Once their plan is approved, students will create their presentations using Prezi and present them to the class. The presentations may be shared with younger grades to help them understand history and periods of time.

Get Real

Prezi is an online presentation tool. This means you'll need the Internet. Always have a backup plan if for some reason your Internet is down on the day students are to present. There's a print feature on Prezi, so when students have their assignment finished, print a copy so you'll have something in case the web is not cooperating. Also,

> The new Web is a communications medium that enables people to create their own content, collaborate with others, and build communities. It has become a tool for self-organization.
>
> —DON TAPSCOTT (2009)

the printed copy will help you keep each presentation in mind when you're scoring the projects.

Focus on content! Prezi pushes students to know their content and to speak about it using key words and images. Requiring students to complete a plan before creating their Prezis allows you to coach them if they don't have a good grasp on the content or if they're focusing only on the details, rather than the main ideas. Make time to check on each student or group of students as they're researching.

We don't want anyone to get motion sick, so model for students how to zoom and move without going overboard. The same features that can make Prezi amazing can also become distracting. Model, model, model examples and have students evaluate the examples to see how much movement is appropriate.

Appendix

References

Allen, R. 2010. *High-Impact Teaching Strategies for the "XYZ" Era of Education*. Boston, MA: Allyn & Bacon.

Callary, J. 2008. "A glimpse into one 1970s textbook." *Tech Trends* 52(5): 15.

Ferriter, B. 2009. "Taking the digital plunge." *Educational Leadership* 67(1): 85–86.

Fitzgerald, M. 2002. "The evolution of technology." *Tech Directions* 61(7): 20–24.

Jensen, E. 2008. "A fresh look at brain-based education." *Phi Delta Kappan,* 89(6).

March, T. 2005/2006. "The new www: whatever, whenever, wherever." *Educational Leadership* 63(4): 14–19.

Marzano, R. 2009. "Teaching with interactive whiteboards." *Educational Leadership* 67(3): 80–82.

http://www.marzanoresearch.com/documents/Continuation_Study_2010.pdf/ (p.35).

Mishra, P., and M. Koehler, 2009. "Too cool for school-no way: Using the TPACK framework you can have hot tools and teach with them too." *Learning and Leading with Technology* 36(7): 14–18.

Mullen, R., and L. Wedwick. 2008. "Avoiding the digital abyss: Getting started in the classroom with YouTube, digital stories, and blogs." *The Clearing House* 82(2): 66–69.

November, A. 2010. *Empowering Students with Technology*. Thousand Oaks, CA: Corwin.

Nussbaum-Beach, S. 2008. "No limits." *Technology and Learning* 28(7): 14–18.

Palfrey, J., and U. Gasser. 2008. *Born Digital: Understanding the First Generation of Digital Natives*. New York: Basic Books.

Plair, S. 2008. "Revamping professional development for technology integration and fluency." *Clearing House* 82(2): 70–74.

Prensky, M. 2001. "Digital natives, digital immigrants." *On the Horizon* 9(5): 1–6.

———. 2010. *Teaching Digital Natives: Partnering for Real Learning.* Thousand Oaks, CA: Corwin.

Richardson, W. 2006. "The Educator's Guide to the Read/Write Web." *Educational Leadership* 63(4): 24–27.

———. 2008. "Footprints." *Educational Leadership* 66(3): 16–19.

Rosen, L. 2010. *Rewired: Understanding the iGeneration and the Way They Learn.* New York: Palgrave & Macmillan.

Sprenger, M. 2010. *Brain-Based Teaching in the Digital Age.* Alexandria, VA: ASCD.

Tapscott, D. 2009. *Grown Up Digital: How the Net Generation Is Changing Your World.* New York: McGraw Hill.

Summary List of Websites

Website	Address
Amazon	http://www.amazon.com/
Animoto	http://animoto.com/
Any Video Converter	http://www.any-video-converter.com/
Audacity	http://audacity.sourceforge.net/
authorSTREAM	http://www.authorstream.com/
Blogger	http://www.blogger.com/
Brain Pop	http://www.brainpop.com/
CNN Student News	http://www.cnn.com/studentnews/
Discovery Education	http://discoveryeducation.com/
Edmodo	http://www.edmodo.com/
Edublogs	http://edublogs.org/
Educational Feeds	http://www.educational-feeds.com/
eI Community	https://www.eicommunity.com/
EPN Web	http://epnweb.org/
Facebook	http://www.facebook.com/
Flickr	http://www.flickr.com/
Garage Band	http://www.apple.com/ilife/garageband/
Glogster	http://edu.glogster.com/
Google Earth	http://www.google.com/earth/
iTunes	http://www.apple.com/itunes/

Website	Address
Live Binders	http://livebinders.com/
Mimio Connect	http://www.mimioconnect.com/
Movavi	http://online.movavi.com/
Newseum	http://www.newseum.org/
Pete's PowerPoint Station	http://pppst.com/
Photo Peach	http://photopeach.com/
Pics 4 Learning	http://www.pics4learning.com/
PodBean	http://www.podbean.com/
Podomatic	http://www.podomatic.com/login/
PowerPoint Games	http://jc-schools.net/tutorials/ppt-games/
Prezi	http://prezi.com/
Promethean Planet	http://www.prometheanplanet.com/
Real Player	http://www.real.com/realplayer/
School Tube	http://www.schooltube.com/
Skype	http://www.skype.com/
Skype an Author Network	http://skypeanauthor.wetpaint.com/
Skype in the Classroom	http://education.skype.com/
Smart Exchange	http://exchange.smarttech.com/
Smilebox	http://www.smilebox.com/
Tagxedo	http://www.tagxedo.com/
Teacher Tube	http://www1.teachertube.com/
Twitter	http://twitter.com/
Vimeo	http://vimeo.com/

Website	Address
Wall Wisher	http://www.wallwisher.com/
Watch Know	http://www.watchknow.org/
Weebly	http://www.weebly.com/
Word Press	http://wordpress.org/
Wordle	http://www.wordle.net/
Yodio	http://www.yodio.com/
YouTube™	http://www.youtube.com/